To Nicole
from
Aunt B
11-05

THE
MOST
IMPORTANT
THING
I KNOW™
ABOUT...

FRIENDSHIP · FAMILY · LOVE · FAITH · KINDNESS
TEACHING · SUCCESS · EXCELLENCE · LEADERSHIP

FROM

**Barbara Bush · The Dalai Lama · Muhammad Ali
and Over 150 Other Eminent Individuals**

THE
MOST
IMPORTANT
THING
I KNOW™
ABOUT...

FRIENDSHIP · FAMILY · LOVE · FAITH · KINDNESS
TEACHING · SUCCESS · EXCELLENCE · LEADERSHIP
FROM
Barbara Bush · The Dalai Lama · Muhammad Ali
and Over 150 Other Eminent Individuals

Lorne A. Adrain

**Andrews McMeel
Publishing**

Kansas City

01 02 03 04 05 RDC 10 9 8 7 6 5 4 3 2 1

Library of Congress Cataloging-in-Publication Data

The most important thing I know about— : friendship, family, love, faith, kindness, teaching, success, excellence, leadership / compiled by Lorne A. Adrain.
      p. cm.
    ISBN 0-7407-1910-6
      1. Conduct of life—Quotations, maxims, etc. 2. Celebrities—Quotations. I. Title:
    Friendship, family, love, faith, kindness, teaching, success, excellence, leadership. II.
      Adrain, Lorne A.

    PN6084.C556 M68 2001
    082—dc21

                                                      2001034091

IN LOVING HONOR OF MY GRANDPARENTS:

James Bernard Gillies
Veronica Eleanor Gillies
Samuel Lorne Adrain
Lilith Elena Adrain

Their good words and works ripple
through my day, lighting the way.

Acknowledgments

T hank you for buying this book. Your purchase will help provide support for many community needs.

Thanks to the generous contributors to this project, those who risked thoughts in the interest of all of us learning something new or seeing something differently or inspiring something good.

Thanks to my wife, Ann, and my children, Ariane, Sam, and Grace, for supporting my dreams. And to my family and friends for encouragement and inspiration and ideas.

Thanks to Christine Rhodes, my hardworking associate in this project, for her dogged determination, her creative energy, her belief in my mission, and her constant optimism. This would not have been possible without her love and dedicated hard work for over a year. To Caroline Carney of BookDeals, Inc., my agent, partner, and friend, whose infectious enthusiasm and gracious good counsel have earned her admirers here and throughout the industry. To Patty Rice of publisher Andrews McMeel, who encouraged and supported and bought this idea!

And to all the people who have inspired me and helped Christine and me with this project in other ways—identifying and finding people, getting them to help, or inspiring dreams of what could be: Joan Abrahamson, Vince Agliata, Sue Aldrich, Dave Amato, Lorraine Bandoni, Bob Beagle, Susanna Beckwith, Dick Butler, Bob Carothers, Billie Faye Curtis, Bonnie Curtis, Debra Dunn, Jamie Koven, Meredith Morse, Phil Pastore, Peter Peduzzi, Mary Ritter, Tom Ruppanner, Rebecca Spencer, and Bobbie-Jean Taylor.

Introduction

I love poking around yard sales, looking for deals, of course, but also imagining the stories and the lessons behind the well-worn articles. It might be an old postcard with a poignant note or an interesting portrait from long ago. From time to time I also come across something that prompts new insights for me. Several years ago I picked up two old books at a local yard sale which did just that. One book, *Leadership*, was a collection of talks given at Harvard University by Bishop Brent of the Philippines in 1907. The second book, *The Aim of Life*, was a collection of talks given to young people by Philip Moxom, and published in 1894. I was compiling my first book at the time and was struck by how similar these ideas and insights from Victorian times were to the messages I had received from contemporary world leaders for my own work. I reminded myself that, as the Bible and other great books have shown us, men and women through the ages have contemplated similar questions about their lives and their worlds and have pursued the same purpose and meaning that we still seek. These great books have provided insight and inspiration around these age-old questions and I hope that my work will contribute in a similar way.

We learn in different ways at different times. Many of life's greatest insights and inspiration are born in the most difficult of circumstances. Others are simply the product of thoughtful observation and a desire to make a difference. Sadly, Viktor E. Frankl died several years ago so I could not ask him to share thoughts with us, but his writing in *Man's Search for Meaning* has been most inspiring for me and offers thoughts remarkably similar in spirit to those shared by leaders in this book. Frankl describes his experience and his most important learning as a prisoner in a Nazi concentration camp—lessons in the enduring power of the human spirit, from heroic prisoners who, despite inhuman conditions, refused to give up their freedom to choose a positive attitude. In that hellish experience he developed other firm beliefs as well: that the spirit of the individual is perhaps the most admirable of all things; that "those held in highest esteem by most people are those who master a hard lot with their head held high"; that "success, like happiness, cannot be pursued, it must ensue, and it only does so as the unintended side-effect of one's personal dedication to a cause greater than oneself"; that "man is ultimately self-determining; man does not simply exist but always decides what his existence will be, what he will become in the next moment . . . every human being has the freedom to change at any instant"; that "when we are no longer able to change a situation, we are challenged to change ourselves." Making the best of a bad situation, as Frankl prescribes, is given further meaning when expressed herein by Kim Phuc. Kim was immortalized as a young girl in the heart-wrenching picture of her painful and frightened run along a village path after having been burned by a napalm bomb in Vietnam. She says, "It's wonderful to . . . live with love and forgiveness." By working for peace and understanding and forgiveness, she has turned her painful experience into a positive lesson for the entire world. Similarly, Máiread Corrigan Maguire, winner of the Nobel Peace Prize, was inspired by tragedy and by the vision of a better world and shares a simple yet most powerful thought with us, "Be kind to all you meet." In 1976, two nephews and a niece, all small children, were killed on a Belfast street corner in the madness of Northern Ireland's struggles. Maguire and her friend Betty Williams founded the Peace People and inspired millions of Irish people to say enough is enough and to dedicate themselves to peacemaking.

In this book you also will hear from many who found inspiration in simply observing possibilities in the world around them and then leading efforts to make the possibilities come alive. George McDonald, a successful businessman in New York City, found himself almost tripping over homeless people on his way to work every day. Profoundly touched by this tragic waste of human potential, McDonald mobilized people and money to establish the Doe Fund, which has helped thousands of people regain their self-esteem and empowered them to become productive members of the community. He says here, "A good leader equips people to care for themselves." Likewise, Wendy Kopp, a senior at Princeton University, was prompted by the inequities in America's education system to start Teach for America, a program that has inspired over six thousand new college graduates to help over five hundred thousand under-privileged students get a better start. Wendy learned so much by looking and listening and caring—a combination that has made untold contributions to lives and to our society.

You will find in these pages many thoughts that are not new, because we know the questions and the lessons to be as old as the hills. But repetition and an infinite number of perspectives help us to absorb them anew, apply them to our lives, and then to share them with others. The thoughts herein on family, friendship, leadership, faith, love, success, excellence, kindness, teaching, and others have been generously given by people all over the world and will, I hope, become touchstones for new ideas, insights, and action in your life.

Inevitably, we each find ourselves in challenging times. Those moments of greatest challenge are also the moments of greatest opportunity for growth of the spirit. Life offers so many possibilities to us all, most notably the freedom to choose our direction at every new moment—to choose to grow our spirit, to lend a hand, to love, and to lead. As Ted Turner advises here, "How much you give is how you keep score." Every day we have opportunities large and small to make little ripples on the pond of life. Our attitude and the little things we choose to say and do every day inspire the behavior of our children, our friends, and our neighbors. Their behavior inspires others who inspire yet others near and far. Our lives—the vision to lead, the courage to create, and the grace to serve—can create positive ripples farther than the eye can see and a spirit that lives far beyond the beating heart.

My hope is that in this book we each will find thoughts and per-spectives igniting new possibilities within us for every circumstance and opportunity we encounter. As the Rev. Peter Gomes of Harvard University shares within these pages, any of us can put "one foot in front of the other, on the way from where you are to where you are meant to be."

Contents

CHAPTER THREE *Teaching*

CHAPTER FOUR *Success and Excellence*

CHAPTER FIVE *Leadership*

CHAPTER ONE

*Friendship,
Family, and Love*

I

The Dalai Lama
Spiritual leader; winner of the Nobel Peace Prize, 1989

> May the frightened cease to be afraid
> And those bound be freed;
> May the weak find power,
> And may their hearts join in friendship.

———————

Tenzin Gyatso ("ocean-like guru") was born in 1935 in Taktser, China, to a peasant family and was designated the fourteenth Dalai Lama in 1937. He was awarded the 1989 Nobel Peace Prize in recognition of his commitment to the nonviolent liberation of Tibet. Through his actions and words, the Dalai Lama is spreading the message of nonviolence, acceptance, and peace throughout the world, teaching a new generation of future leaders the importance of kindness in all facets of life.

THE DALAI LAMA

༢ ཐུགས་རྗེ་ཆེན་པོ་འཕགས་མཆོག་སྤྱན་རས་གཟིགས།

འཇམ་དཔལ་དབྱངས་དང་གསང་བདག་ཕྱག་ན་རྡོ།

མགོན་པོ་ཚེ་དཔག་མེད་དང་རྣམ་པར་རྒྱལ།

འཆི་མེད་གཙུག་ཏོར་དྲི་མེད་རྣམ་རྒྱལ་མ།

བཅས་ལ་འདུད།

ཕྱག་འཚལ་བཀྲ་ཤིས་བདེ་ལེགས།

2
YOKO ONO
Musician; artist

Imagine!

Yoko Ono earned a degree in philosophy from Tokyo's Gakushuin University, and went on to study philosophy and music at Sarah Lawrence College in New York. Ono has been a pioneer in performance art. She met her husband, John Lennon, at her own one-woman, avant-garde art show in London in 1966. Now in her sixties, she continues to push the creative envelope.

Imagine!

love.
yoko ono

3
GLORIA STEINEM
Women's leader; founder of MS. *magazine*

A friend is chosen family.

Gloria Steinem embraced the surge of feminism in the late 1960s, and with Bella Abzug, Shirley Chisholm, and Betty Friedan, Steinem formed the National Women's Political Caucus to promote women's voting in the 1972 elections. Also in 1972, Steinem founded MS. magazine. Steinem serves as an inspiration to young women around the nation, encouraging education, awareness, and peaceful activism.

Gloria Steinem

A friend is chosen
family —

Gloria Steinem

4
Baba Amte
Religious leader; winner of the Templeton Award, 1990

Love alone can resurrect any man in agony.

Born into a wealthy Brahmin Indian family in the Warora District in the Maharashtra State in India in 1914, Murlindhar Devidas Baba Amte could easily have spent his life pursuing leisure and been secure in his financial future. Instead, Amte found his fortune in helping fellow citizens who many of his countrymen considered to be the lowest form of humans. Through a lifetime of service to some of the world's most downtrodden people, Murlindhar Devidas Baba Amte personifies selfless charity.

Love alone can
resurrect any man
in agony.
2·8·99   Baba Amte

Anandwan: A Sanctuary of
                Love and
poem in action

5
BERNARD S. SIEGEL, M.D.
Author; oncologist

> The most important thing I know about family is that there
> is only one family. We all have the same parents, are the
> same color inside and, therefore, are all related. Accept,
> love, forgive and become one.

––––––––––

When the Yale-trained surgeon published his first book, *Love, Medicine, and Miracles*, in 1987, it was a huge success, and was acknowledged as a groundbreaking book on mind-body healing, a new idea at that time. Bernie Siegel usually writes books about exceptional people who are suffering or face other great challenges, believing that their struggles provide lessons for us all. His work in helping others reminds each of us to live fully and appreciate what is really important.

Bernard S. Siegel, MD.

The most important thing I
know about family is that
there is only one family.
We all have the same
parents, are the same color
inside and, therefore, are all
related.
Accept, love, forgive and
become one.

Bernie Siegel, MD

6
HELEN GURLEY BROWN
Author; editor; publisher

The more people you fit in to your circle of love the more love there is for everybody in the circle . . . you don't even have to ration . . . there is always enough love to go around.

———————————

Propelled to fame with her best-selling book *Sex and the Single Girl* (1962), Helen Gurley Brown became editor of a floundering Hearst publication called *Cosmopolitan.* She gave it a complete makeover, and brought it from obscurity to lasting success and popularity, helping young women around the world to achieve success professionally, socially, and financially.

The more people you fit in to
your circle of love the more love there
is for every Body in the circle ...
You don't even have to ration ...
there is always enough love
to go around

Helen Gurley Brown

7
SARGENT SHRIVER
First director of the Peace Corps; president of Special Olympics International

The most important thing I know about living is love. Nothing surpasses the benefits received by a human being who makes compassion and love the objective of his or her life. For it is only by compassion and love that anyone fulfills successfully their own life's journey. Nothing equals love. Only God surpasses it, a power which He demonstrated by His life on earth and by His loving commitment to each one of us, and to all of us, whom He has created and put together here on His earth.

––––––––

Robert Sargent Shriver Jr. graduated Yale Law School in 1940 and married Eunice Kennedy, with whom he founded the Special Olympics. He gained national prominence as the first director of the Peace Corps, one of the most popular initiatives of the Kennedy administration. Later he served President Nixon as ambassador to France and ran for vice-president with Senator George McGovern in 1972.

The most important thing I know about living is love. Nothing surpasses the benefits received by a human being who makes compassion and love the objective of his or her life. For it is only by compassion and love that anyone fulfills successfully their own life's journey. Nothing equals love. Only God surpasses it, a power which He demonstrated by His life on earth and by His loving commitment to each one of us, and to all of us, whom He has created & put together here on His earth.

Sargent Shriver

8
NANCY CLARK, M.S., R.D.
Nutritionist

The friendships you make while participating in sports are the chocolate chips in this cookie called life.

Nancy Clark, M.S., R.D., is an internationally known sports nutritionist and nutrition author. Her more renowned clients include members of the Boston Red Sox, the Boston Celtics, the New England Blizzard (women's professional basketball team), and many Olympic athletes. She also serves as part of the training team for the Leukemia and Lymphoma Society's Team in Training program, through which non-professional athletes train for and run a marathon to raise money for a cure.

The friendships you make while
participating in sports are the
chocolate chips in this cookie called life.

Nancy Clark

9
GEORGE W. BUSH
Forty-third president of the United States

I have been given the greatest gift by two wonderful
parents: unconditional love.

Born in 1946 in New Haven, Connecticut, to Barbara and George
Herbert Walker Bush, George W. is a graduate of Harvard Business
School, a successful business leader, the first Texas governor to be
elected to consecutive four-year terms, and winner of the closest
presidential election in U.S. history. A "compassionate conservative," Bush has worked for a government that balances constructive
involvement in people's lives with an equally beneficial detachment
from them.

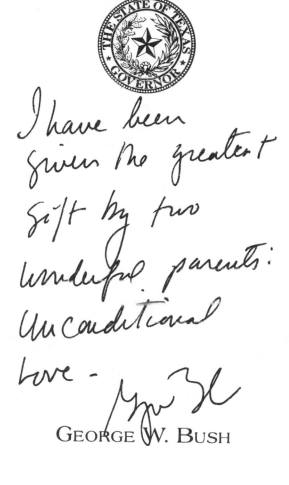

I have been
given the greatest
gift by two
wonderful parents:
Unconditional
Love -

GEORGE W. BUSH

10
Barbara Bush
First lady of the United States

> From birth to death our first responsibility on earth is to our
> families . . . immediate and extended. They are our joy,
> love, friends, strength, and our responsibility. A country is
> only as strong as its families.

Former First Lady of the United States Barbara Bush has had an important impact on the lives of Americans. After losing a daughter at age three to leukemia, she became an advocate for children with leukemia and is best known, perhaps, for her work in family literacy. Bush champions her belief that if more people were able to read and express themselves through writing, many of the social problems in the United States and around the world would be resolved.

Barbara Bush

From birth to death our first responsibility on earth is to our family ... immediate and extended. They are our joy, love, friends, strength and <u>our responsibility</u>. A country is only as strong as it's families.

Barbara Bush

11
ROBERT SCHULLER
Religious leader

Love is my decision to make your problem my concern.

Robert Schuller's weekly *Hour of Power* is the most broadly televised church service in the world. Garden Grove, California, still hosts his original congregation, now with over ten thousand members, and worshiping in the famous Crystal Cathedral, constructed entirely of glass. Schuller has written thirty-two books in all, and is sought after for his charismatic speaking style and motivational abilities.

ROBERT SCHULLER

Love is my
decision to
make your
problem my
concern RvtHua

12
HELEN THOMAS
White House reporter, covered six presidents

> Love means giving unconditionally. It knows no limits. It is
> the most humanizing of all feelings.

Helen Thomas was the first woman to be White House bureau chief
for a newswire service, the first woman president of the White House
Correspondents Association, and the first woman officer of the
National Press Club. She covered six presidents, beginning with
President Kennedy and ending with President Clinton.

HELEN THOMAS

*Love means giving
unconditionally. It
knows no limits.
It is the most
human of all
feelings.*

*Helen Thomas
UPI White
House Reporter*

Front Row at the White House

13
Daniel Zingale
AIDS leader; executive director, AIDS Action

In the most horrific experiences of humankind, love not only endures, it thrives.

The executive director of AIDS Action, named by the *New York Times* as "among the country's most powerful advocacy groups," Daniel Zingale heads a network of 3,200 national AIDS service organizations and the one million HIV-positive Americans they serve.

In the most horrific
experiences of
humankind, love not
only endures,
it thrives.

                    Daniel Zingale

14
BETTY FORD
First lady of the United States

Unconditional love is the greatest gift you can give to yourself or to another.

Betty Ford is widely admired as an outspoken supporter of equal rights and reproductive rights for women and is perhaps best known worldwide for her dignity, honesty, and strength during her treatment for breast cancer, and later for alcoholism. In 1982, following her own treatment for her alcoholism, she founded the Betty Ford Center in California and has been credited with destigmatizing the disease of alcoholism and encouraging education and treatment programs for alcoholics and families of alcoholics.

BETTY FORD

" Unconditional love is the greatest gift you can give to yourself or to another "

Betty Ford

15
JANE GOODALL
Animal rights leader

I have found that to love and be loved is the most
empowering and exhilarating of all human emotions: so
when the bond is broken, through death or betrayal, the
grief and spiritual devastation is all but unendurable.

———————

Reason for Hope, Jane Goodall's autobiography, underscores her
commitment to primate welfare and environmental protection. For
nearly ten years she studied the rarely observed lives of chimpanzees and established chimpanzee sanctuaries for the care and
rehabilitation of orphaned chimpanzees in four African countries.
Through her speaking, her actions, and her work with children, she
demonstrates that we each make a difference every day and that our
ability to make a difference is our reason for hope.

The Jane Goodall Institute

I have found that to love and
be loved is the most empowering
and exhilarating of all human
emotions: so when the bond is
broken, through death or betrayal,
the grief and spiritual devastation
is all but unendurable

Jane Goodall

© Mark Maglio 1990

"Fifi fishing for termites"
derived from Hugo Van Lawick, 1964 photo.

16
YOLANDA KING
Civil rights leader; actor

> To love and be loved is the greatest gift you can give and
> the most awesome blessing to receive!

Yolanda King is the oldest child of Martin Luther King Jr. and Coretta
Scott King; she has used her talent for acting and performing to
remember and honor the work of her father. As an actor, King has
devoted herself to effecting social and personal change throughout
the arts by integrating her artistic goals with human rights causes.

Yolanda King

To love and be loved
is the greatest gift you
Can give and the most
awesome blessing to receive!

Yolanda King

17
TORSTEN WIESEL
Winner of the Nobel Prize in physiology or medicine, 1981

The essence of love
Respect
Generosity
Passion

Torsten Wiesel performed pioneering research at Harvard on the visual cortex of the brain. He and collaborator David Hubel shared the 1981 Nobel Prize in physiology or medicine for their discovery of how the brain interprets the messages it receives from the eyes.

The essence of love
Respect
Generosity
Passion

Torsten Wiesel

18

NORA ROBERTS
Writer; international best-seller

Love, very simply, matters most.

———————

Nora Roberts has come a long way since writing her first romance novel in a spiral notebook with a #2 pencil. She has broken all the old barriers in romance writing and has taken the genre from obscurity to blockbusting fame. She has published over 130 novels, all best-sellers, and at one time had eleven titles simultaneously on the *New York Times* hardcover and paperback best-seller lists.

Nora Roberts

Love, very simply, matters
most.

Nora Roberts

19

RALPH E. REED JR.
Political leader, the Christian Coalition

> True love is when you give up your own selfish preferences,
> desires, and wants in order to accept someone for who they
> are, not what you want them to be.

Ralph E. Reed Jr. founded Students for America, became its executive director, and built a grassroots conservative student network. Reed was the executive director of the Christian Coalition from its inception in 1989 until 1997. He is widely acknowledged to be one of the most influential forces in American politics.

True love is when you give up your own selfish preferences, desires, and wants in order to accept someone for who they are, not what you want them to be.

20

BRIGITTE BARDOT
Actor, animal rights leader

> Love brings us closer to perfection. It is the sun that lights
> up our life and warms that of others. I love you!

———————————

Brigitte Bardot appeared on the cover of *Elle* magazine at the age of
fifteen and immediately captured the imagination of the fashion and
film worlds. Since retiring from her film career, she has been an
activist for animal rights worldwide, lending her notoriety to the
causes of protecting animals from being used in the testing of beauty
products and other inhumane medical experiments.

1999

L'amour nous rapproche de la perfection.

C'est le soleil qui illumine notre vie et réchauffe celle des autres.

Je t'aime!

Brigitte Bardot

21
ERNEST J. GAINES
Writer

For me, love is compassion for mankind, respect of nature:
the lack of either makes life an obscenity.

Ernest J. Gaines has distinguished himself as an American writer,
reflecting poignantly the African American experience as he lived it in
his rural Louisiana childhood. Gaines's most acclaimed work, *The
Autobiography of Miss Jane Pittman*, reveals the quiet dignity and
strength of character that can flourish in anyone.

Ernest J. Gaines

For me, love is Compassion
for mankind, respect of Nature:
the lack of either makes life
an Obscenity.

Ernest J. Gaines

22

SANDRA R. SCANTLING
Therapist—sex, intimacy, and relationships

The sweetness of lasting intimacy grows out of the rockier
terrain of self-discovery . . . Before you can be intimate with
another, you must first dare to be intimate with yourself.

———————

Helping couples improve their intimacy has been Sandra Scantling's
passion for more than twenty years. As a highly respected psy-
chotherapist and certified sex therapist, Scantling has used her experience with thousands of individuals and couples to write two books
and an acclaimed video series called Ordinary Couples, Extraordinary
Sex, which has sold nearly a million copies worldwide.

Sandra R. Scantling

The sweetness of lasting Intimacy
Grows out of the rockier terrain
Of self discovery --- Before you
Can be intimate with another,
You must first dare to be intimate
with Yourself.

Sandra Scantling

23

THOMAS MOORE
Writer; theologian

The Greek poet Sappho described love as bittersweet.
It creates and destroys. Its mystery is as deep as its power
is strong. Still, it is worth every risk.

———————

In his two best-selling books, *Care of the Soul* and *Soul Mates*,
Catholic monk and author Thomas Moore urges his readers to do as
he does and search for the sacred in every moment, in each day. He
sets out three basic principles for a full and spiritually fulfilling life:
simplify, see the importance of vibrancy and color, and practice being
spiritual.

THOMAS MOORE

The Greek poet Sappho described love
as bittersweet. It creates and destroys.
Its mystery is as deep as its power is
strong. Still, it is worth every risk.

The Moore

24

CANDACE LIGHTNER

Community leader; cofounder of Mothers Against Drunk Driving (MADD)

> Love should be given unselfishly and without expectations, otherwise you continually will be disappointed.

––––––––––––––––

Twenty years ago, Candace Lightner, a grieving mother, began a grassroots organization to campaign against drunk driving, the cause of her daughter's death. Mothers Against Drunk Driving (MADD) played a substantial role in reducing such fatalities by 40 percent in twenty years. MADD has become a potent model for other advocacy start-up groups across the country, and Lightner is a shining example of the power of one to make a difference.

From the desk of
    Candace Lightner

Love should be given unselfishly
and without expectations, otherwise
you continually will be disappointed
                Candace Lightner
                Founder / MADD

25
RICHARD ANDERSON
Actor

There is nothing like it . . . once you have found it . . . love.

Richard Anderson began his acting career with the likes of Spencer Tracy, Cary Grant, William Holden, Clark Gable, and Walter Pidgeon but is perhaps best-remembered as Oscar Goldman, from *The Six Million Dollar Man,* starring Lee Majors. Anderson was nominated for an Oscar and made twenty-nine films during the height of his film career, including Stanley Kubrick's *Paths of Glory,* which has since become an antiwar film classic. A longtime spokesperson for the *Kiplinger Washington Newsletter,* Anderson also is devoted to the California Indian Manpower Consortium, to help advance education and job training for Native Americans.

RICHARD ANDERSON

There is nothing like
it... once you have
found it... love.

Richard Anderson

26
Ilya Prigogine
Winner of the Nobel Prize in chemistry, 1977

> Love shatters the barriers between the ego and the outside
> world. It expresses our longing to belong to the human
> world and the world of nature.

———————————

Ilya Prigogine was awarded the Nobel Prize in chemistry in 1977 for his contributions to nonequilibrium thermodynamics, particularly the theory of dissipative structures. Prigogine serves as special advisor to the European community in Brussels and as honorary member of the World Commission of Culture and Development of UNESCO, through which he shares his knowledge of statistical mathematics and chemistry for the betterment of societies around the globe.

Le Vicomte et la Vicomtesse Prigogine

Love shatters the barriers between
the ego and the outside world.
It expresses our longing to belong
to the human world and the
world of nature

      Maxine and Ilya
        Prigogine

27
ANN RICHARDS
Governor of Texas

> When everything is darkest, your family will be there for
> you. Tell them how much you love them.

An active Democrat, Ann Richards was elected county commissioner
and state treasurer in Texas before becoming the first female governor of Texas since Ma Ferguson (1933–1935). Although her early
career was complicated by alcoholism, she entered recovery and
gained national respect for overcoming her personal challenge and
for her rousing nomination speeches at the Democratic National
Conventions in 1988 and 1992.

When everything is darkest, your family will be there for you. Tell them how much you love them.

Ann Richards

28

RAY CONNIFF
Musician

> The real meaning of Christmas is the giving of love every
> day.

Ray Conniff's musical contributions have been striking a chord with the public for over fifty years. Conniff was born in 1916 to local musicians in Attleboro, Massachusetts. Conniff recorded one hundred albums, sold sixty-five million records, received a Grammy, and has become one of the world's most beloved artists.

THE REAL MEANING OF CHRISTMAS

WORDS — MUSIC BY
RAY CONNIFF

The real meaning of
Christmas is the
giving of love every day.
Ray Conniff

29
MRS. NORMAN VINCENT PEALE
Religious leader; chair of the board, Guideposts

Love is the most wonderful emotion anyone can have. To
be genuine it must come from the heart. Then it permeates
the entire body.

Love brings many rewards. It helps to create a feeling of
self-worth. It motivates a giving spirit. It enhances a
peaceful life. It helps to make living a great experience.

Ruth Stafford Peale is a religious leader, motivational speaker, and
author. She serves communities across the United States and around
the globe with her message that faith can work powerfully in ordinary
lives. She is cofounder, publisher, and chair of the board of
Guideposts. The organization is unified around helping people from all
walks of life achieve their maximum personal and spiritual potential.

Love is the most wonderful emotion anyone can have. To be genuine it must come from the heart. Then it permeates the entire body.

Love brings many rewards. It helps to create a feeling of self-worth. It motivates a giving spirit. It enhances a peaceful life. It helps to make living a great experience.

Ruth Stafford Peale

30
DON MURRAY
Actor

> Love is not an emotion; it's a devotion of one's time,
> attention and resources to the benefit of another.

Best remembered for his Oscar-nominated performance as the naive
cowboy who romances Marilyn Monroe in *Bus Stop*, Don Murray is an
actor and performer who used his talents and the movie industry for
social causes. In his screen messages and in his life, Murray
inspires people to reach out a hand in love—for troubled juveniles,
for people with diseases, for people different from ourselves.

Love is not an emotion;
it's a devotion
of one's time, attention
and resources
to the benefit of another

Dan Murray

31
BRENDA LEE
Musician; country music star

> Love rejoices in the good that happens to others. Above all
> else, love never fails.

Born in 1944, Brenda Lee sang her way out of an impoverished childhood and into the hearts of the world. After nearly forty-five years in
the music industry, Lee still sings to sold-out audiences. She has
received four Grammy nominations, won numerous awards, and sold
more records—over 100 million—than any other woman in the history of recorded music. In addition to her music career, Lee gives a
great deal to the larger community as a leading volunteer for numerous charitable organizations.

Love rejoices in the good that happens to others. Above all else, love never fails.

Brenda Lee

32
JEFF GETTY
AIDS activist

Love was always the road I was traveling upon when
I realized I exist, in part, as God.

In the mid 1980s, then thirty-nine-year-old Jeff Getty discovered he was
HIV-positive and began working tirelessly with AIDS awareness organizations. In 1996, Getty became the first human to receive an experi-
mental transplant of baboon bone marrow, an experiment in boosting
the immune system. His courageous act was one of many in his efforts
to help put a stop to one of the world's most deadly diseases.

JEFF GETTY

AIDS ACTIVIST

Love was always the road I was traveling upon when I realized I exist, in-port, as God.

Jeff Getty

33
ART LINKLETTER
Entertainer; author; radio broadcaster; entrepreneur

Rogers and Hammerstein said it best—
A song is not a song—until you sing it—
A bell is not a bell—until you ring it—
Love was not put in your heart to stay
For love is not love 'til you give it away.

———————————

Born in Moosejaw, Sasketchewan, Canada, Art Linkletter began his life abandoned by his parents on the doorsteps of a local church. He was adopted by an itinerant preacher and his wife, who encouraged his love for broadcasting. Linkletter became known for his ability to entertain his audience through the actions of ordinary people and leveraged that talent into books and television shows that captured the hearts of all America.

Rodgers and Hammerstein said it
best —

A song is not a song — until you sing it —
A bell is not a bell — until you ring it —
Love was not put in your heart to stay
For Love is not Love 'Til you give it away.

Art Linkletter

34
MILLARD FULLER
Philanthropist

> Love motivates. Love inspires! Love ignites!! Love is
> awesome!!!

As the founder of Habitat for Humanity International, Millard Fuller
has led an initiative that became one of the most successful service
projects in the world. Habitat for Humanity has helped over 350,000
people move into homes built by volunteers. Fuller is an extraordinary
example of the power and possibility of one person's vision to change
the world around him, one step at a time.

Love motivates,
Love inspires!
Love ignites!!
Love is awesome !!!

Millard Fuller

35
HAL DAVID
Musician

What the world needs now is love is more than a title of one of my songs. It's what I believe each of us would and should share with others.

————————

An extraordinarily gifted songwriter, Hal David's music is loved around the world by people of all ages. Often working with Burt Bacharach, David has held a prominent spot in Hollywood's music-movie industry for decades. Their work together has been original, heartfelt, and universally enjoyed.

What the world needs now
is *love* is more than a
trifle of me of my soup, it's
that I believe each *Jus*
want to should share
with me another
(signature)

36
ANDREW WEIL, M.D.
Health and healing research

You can only love others to the extent that you can love yourself.

―――――――――――

Acclaimed author and world-renowned integrative medicine pioneer Andrew Weil has made a huge impact on the way people think about healing, health, and the interactions between mind and body. He earned degrees in botany and medicine from Harvard University and, as a Fellow of the Institute of Current World Affairs, travels through-out the world researching medicinal plants and healing to advance the science of medicine.

ANDREW WEIL, MD

YOU CAN ONLY LOVE
OTHERS TO THE EXTENT
THAT YOU CAN LOVE
YOURSELF.

37
SISTER HELEN PREJEAN
Death penalty opponent; author of Dead Man Walking

Love is the energy of God. Pray for it. Lavish it on others, receive it gratefully when it comes to you. Cultivate friendship like a garden. It is the best love of all.

While living in the St. Thomas Housing Project in New Orleans, Sister Prejean agreed to be a pen pal to a man on death row. This would change her life in ways that she could not have imagined. In April 1984, Sister Helen witnessed the death by electrocution of Patrick Sonnier, to whom she served as spiritual adviser for the months leading up to his execution. She wrote of this life-altering experience in *Dead Man Walking,* which was a national best-seller, was nominated for the Pulitzer Prize, was made into a critically acclaimed film, and advanced the debate on abolition of the death penalty.

66

Love is the energy of God.
Pray for it, lavish it on others,
receive it gratefully when it
comes to you. Cultivate
friendship like a garden.
It is the best love of all. "

Sister Helen Prejean, csj

38
THEODORE BIKEL
Actor

You give love in order to give, not in order to get.

Best known for his role as Georg von Trapp in Rodgers and Hammerstein's Broadway musical *The Sound of Music* (1959), Theodore Bickel was born in Vienna, Austria, in 1924. It is his portrayal of Georg von Trapp, the father seeking to escape communism and hatred, to love and protect his family, that helps to define Bikel's feelings about the exponential powers of giving love away unselfishly, for the benefit of others.

Theodore Bikel

You give love
in order to give
Not in order to get

39
JEFF FOXWORTHY
Comic

True happiness doesn't come from "things." It comes from love. Love of God, family, friends, strangers and self.

Jeff Foxworthy's four CD releases have tallied sales of over eight million units, making him the biggest selling comedy recording artist in history. Foxworthy is a tireless volunteer for children with cancer and provides fund-raising leadership on the issue on behalf of the Duke University Children's Hospital in Durham, North Carolina.

True happiness doesn't come from "things". It comes from love. Love of God, family, friends, strangers and self.

Jeff Foxworthy

40
KRESKIN
Performer, "The Amazing Kreskin"

> To me, "Love" proves that man can communicate
> "telepathically" without the use of our five senses

At age eleven, Kreskin received permission to study the entire psychology section of his local library. Soon he began to perform professionally, billed as "The World's Youngest Hypnotist." Kreskin maintains that silent communication is within the capability of many people, once trained and self sensitized. "Basically, I apply the power of positive thinking, which may be mankind's ultimate tool."

KRESKIN

To me, "Love"

proves that man can communicate

"telepathically" without the use of our

five senses.

Especially,

Kreskin

41
ARLENE DAHL
Actor

> Take each other for better or worse but never for granted
> should be added to the marriage vows, then love would
> blossom every day.

Arlene Dahl made twenty-six movies in her five-decade career as a
Hollywood actor. She was one of the most popular actors in the world
during the post-WWII period. After retiring from films, Dahl became a
successful columnist, writer, and entrepreneur.

Arlene Lahe

Take each other
for better or worse
but never for granted
should be added to
the marriage vows then
love would blossom
every day.

Arlene Lahe

42
Rosa Parks
Civil rights pioneer

I can see a better world because it exists today in small pockets of this country and in a small pocket of every person's heart.

On December 1, 1955, Rosa Parks refused to give up her seat to a white male passenger on a segregated Montgomery bus. Her arrest for failing to do so led to a 381-day boycott, which led to the Supreme Court declaring segregation unconstitutional. For her role in the anti-segregation movement, Parks earned recognition as the "mother" of the civil rights revolution. In 1999, Parks received the Congressional Gold Medal.

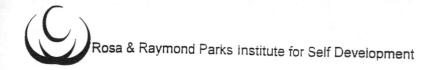Rosa & Raymond Parks Institute for Self Development

I can see a better world because it exists today in small pockets of this country and in a small pocket of every person's heart.

Rosa L. Parks

43

FREDERIK WILLEM (F. W.) DE KLERK
President of South Africa; winner of the Nobel Peace Prize, 1993

The true meaning of love lies in giving and not in receiving.

As president of South Africa, de Klerk led the difficult work of dismantling apartheid. The culmination of apartheid's repeal was the signing of a new constitutional agreement with Nelson Mandela, whom he had freed after twenty-seven years of imprisonment. De Klerk and Mandela were jointly awarded the Nobel Peace Prize, sending a clear message that the hope of civilization rests on the courage in each of us to do what is right and fair, against all odds, for the good of one and all.

The true meaning
of love lies in
giving and not
in receiving.

F.W. deKlerk.

CHAPTER TWO

Faith and Kindness

44
MÁIREAD CORRIGAN MAGUIRE
Winner of the Nobel Peace Prize, 1976; founder of Peace People

Be kind to all you meet.

From 1969 to 1998, over 3,400 people were killed in a brutal war stemming from British colonial interests, revolutionary republicanism, and age-old, oppressive religious bigotry. Thousands of ordinary people throughout Northern Ireland, mainly women, had been calling for an end to the killings and a future of peace for Ireland. Máiread Corrigan Maguire stood at the heart of these people for peace, and organized the largest nonviolent demonstrations in the history of Northern Ireland. Maguire shared the 1976 Nobel Peace Prize for her work toward peace.

PEACE PEOPLE

With Compliments

Be kind to all you meet.
Shalom,
Máiread Corrigan Maguire

45
LUIS PALAU
Religious leader

"For God so loved the world that He gave his one and only son, so that whoever believes in Him shall not perish, but have eternal life." St. John, 3:16

Luis Palau is the author of more than one hundred articles and forty-four books in English and Spanish, including *Where Is God When Bad Things Happen?* and *God Is Relevant.* During more than thirty years of mass evangelism, Palau has spoken to hundreds of millions of people in 104 nations through radio and television broadcasts, and face-to-face to thirteen million people in sixty-eight nations. Featured in a *Wall Street Journal* article in November 1995 as "The Billy Graham of Everywhere," Palau intends to carry his message of faith in God and world peace to all nations for many years to come.

LUIS PALAU

" For God so loved
the world that He
gave his one and only
Son, so that whoever
believes in Him shall
not perish, but have
eternal life " —
St. John 3:16

46
KIM PHUC
Advocate for peace

It's wonderful to know Jesus Christ as my personal savior
and to live with love and forgiveness.

Kim Phuc is best known as the young girl running up a dirt road in
Vietnam, her skin on fire from napalm. That photograph, taken June 8,
1972, was printed on front pages of newspapers around the world,
and may have changed the course of the war in Vietnam and the way
that society looks at all wars. Phuc is now a Canadian citizen and a
United Nations Goodwill Ambassador; she travels the world to recount
her life story of forgiveness and peace.

KIM PHUC

It's wonderful to know
JESUS CHRIST as my personal
savior and to live with
love and forgiveness.

Kim Phuc

KIM PHUC PHAN THI

47
Capt. Scott O'Grady
U.S. Air Force F-16 pilot

True happiness in life comes from our relationship with God and the people we love.

Air Force captain Scott O'Grady was shot down over Bosnia and hid from enemy soldiers in the underbrush for six days. O'Grady says that during his descent under his bright parachute, which felt like a neon sign announcing his arrival, these three things became the most important things for him—faith, the love of his family, and his love of America. He brushes off being called a hero and says the biggest hero today is a parent who teaches his or her children good values and loves them unconditionally.

Capt. Scott O'Grady
U.S. Air Force F-16 pilot
Bosnian War survivor
2 to 8 June 1995

True happiness in Life
comes from our relationship
with GOD and the people
we Love.

GOD Bless

Scott O'Grady

"Basher 52"

12 OCT 2000
(Birthday)

48
JANET LEIGH
Actor

Love is the showing forth of the very self of God!

Janet Leigh is best known for her part in the Alfred Hitchcock thriller *Psycho*, which earned her a Golden Globe Award and a nomination for Best Supporting Actress at the 1960 Academy Awards. She acted in more than fifty movies and is among America's favorite stars of all time.

Janet Leigh

Love is the showing
forth of the very
Self of God!

Janet Leigh

49
JAYNE TORVILL
Athlete, Olympic figure skater

Be honest with yourself and with others.

———————

Jayne Torvill was born in 1957 in Nottingham, Nottinghamshire, England. Along with partner Christopher Dean, Torvill was world ice-dance champion from 1981 to 1984 and won the Olympic gold medal in 1984. Their highly acclaimed performances included an interpretation of music from Ravel's *Bolero*. They reappeared at the Olympics in 1994 and won the bronze medal.

Jayne Torvill OBE

Be honest with yourself and
with others,

Jayne Torvill

50
WALLY LAMB
Writer; educator

Love sprouts from the rich loam of forgiveness. Mongrels
make good dogs. The evidence of God exists in the
roundness of things. This much, at least, I've figured out. I
know this much is true.

Wally Lamb's first novel, *She's Come Undone*, received rave reviews
when it was published in 1992. His most recent novel, *I Know This
Much Is True,* has also been a best-seller. Lamb creates compelling
characters and situations that enable his readers to identify with and
understand people they might not otherwise try to accept. In this
way, Lamb is closing gaps among people, minimizing our differences,
and accentuating our similarities—our common needs for love,
acceptance, and belonging.

Wally Lamb, Novelist

Love sprouts from the rich loam of forgiveness: Mongrels make good dogs. The evidence of ~~God~~ exists in the roundness of things. This much, at least, I've figured out. I know this much is true.

Wally Lamb

51
GERALYN WOLF
Episcopal bishop, Diocese of Rhode Island

> The important thing I know about faith is that it is not
> something to hold on to, but to be held by.

———————

Bishop Gerry Wolf has the distinct honor of being one of only eleven
female Bishops in the Episcopal Church worldwide. She was the first
female dean of an Episcopal cathedral, elected in 1987 at Christ
Church Cathedral, Louisville, Kentucky. She says that she has often
thought of her ministry as a wedge plowing a field that is hard, leaving behind something softer that is ready for new life. She is a pioneer, making the road easier for those who will follow her.

the episcopal diocese of rhode island
office of the bishop

The important thing I know about
faith is that it is not something to
hold on to, but to be held by.

+ Geralyn Wolf

52
RABBI HAROLD S. KUSHNER
Religious leader; author

To me, faith has always meant giving God the benefit of the doubt, living and acting on the assumption that the world is hospitable to honesty, generosity and kindness.

In 1981, Rabbi Harold S. Kushner brought the American public a new way to look at tragedy with his best-seller *When Bad Things Happen to Good People*. Since that time, the book has been translated into twelve different languages. In 1995, Kushner was awarded the Christopher Medal for his book *When All You've Ever Wanted Isn't Enough,* and he was honored as one of the fifty people who helped make the world a better place in the last fifty years.

To me, faith has always meant giving God the benefit of the doubt, living and acting on the assumption that the world is hospitable to honesty, generosity and kindness.

Harold Kushner

53
HEATHER WHITESTONE
Miss America, 1995; first deaf Miss America

With faith and God, the impossible is indeed possible. John 3:16

Heather Whitestone became the first deaf Miss America when she was crowned at age twenty-three. Her courage in participating in the pageant and her dignity in bringing the issues of deaf people to the forefront have helped all of us accept and support one another's differences.

With faith and God, the
impossible is indeed possible.

John 3:16

Heather Whitestone
Miss America 1995

54
JACK KORNFIELD
Author, inspirational best-sellers

In the end, you never regret being kind.

———————————

Jack Kornfield, Ph.D., is a clinical psychologist, therapist, author of six books, and founder of the Spirit Rock Center in Woodacre, California. The classical teachings of Buddha, which Kornfield brings to his writing, his students, and his own life, stress the central role of mindfulness and awareness in developing a life of wisdom and compassion. He brings his message around the world through his books, instructional tapes, and retreats in order to foster acceptance, peace, and kindness.

Spirit Rock
Meditation
Center

...in the Buddhist tradition

In the end, you
never regret being
kind.

Jack
Kornfield

55
ORAL ROBERTS
Religious leader; university founder

Never doubt . . . the power of your own faith!

An Evangelist and faith healer born in Ada, Oklahoma, Oral Roberts continues, after decades of preaching, to have a substantial impact on religious thinking throughout the world. He founded Oral Roberts University in 1967 and continues spreading the message of faith, fellowship, acceptance, and healing that has earned him the highest regard within a variety of religious communities.

ORAL ROBERTS
UNIVERSITY

Oral Roberts
Founder/Chancellor

Never doubt . . .
The power 2 your
own faith!

Oral Roberts

56
Bonnie Guiton Hill
Foundation president

"To be grateful for past blessings leads to the door for future blessings. Faith opens the door."

As president and CEO of the Times Mirror Foundation, Bonnie Hill is responsible for developing and promoting the company's philanthropic initiatives. Hill shares her experiences as a leader in business and philanthropic endeavors with other women around the country who are interested in pursuing careers and lives like hers, dedicated to improving our communities through education, growth in business, and charitable work.

Bonnie Guiton Hill

"To be grateful for past
blessings leads to the
door for future blessings.
Faith opens the door."

Bonnie Hill

57
MARIA VON TRAPP
Subject of The Sound of Music

America is a big country with wide, open spaces and that reflects all the people. Americans have a big wide heart when they come in contact with needs of others. This is what we "The Trapp Family Singers" experienced when we came to this country in 1938. They opened their homes, lent us their car to explore around, took us on holiday trips to the Catskills and for a swim to cool off during the hot summer in Philadelphia and, and . . . and came to Vermont to help us build our new house. When we started Austrian Relief, they stuffed our bus with everything one would need: clothes, shoes, coats, food, and care packages by the arms full. Yes, we experienced the genuine generosity of America. When people overseas complain about the loud-behaved Americans, I tell them: "Come to America and learn from their Big-Wide Heart."

Maria von Trapp is one of the of the von Trapp family, made famous in *The Sound of Music*. She applied much of her life's work in Papua, New Guinea, carrying out her father Capt. Georg von Trapp's teachings of faith, honor, duty, and love through service to others. Von Trapp continues to play her music and remains a tireless world traveler for peace.

The Spirit of America

America is a big country with wide, open spaces and that reflects on the people. Americans have a big, wide heart when they come in contact with needs of others.

This is what we "The Trapp Family Singers" experienced when we came to this country in 1938.

They opened their homes, lend us their car to explore around, took us on holiday trips to the Catskills and for a swim in the Rancocas to cool off during the hot Summers in Philadelphia and, and .... and came to Vermont to help us build our new home.

When we started "Austrian Relief" they stuffed our bus with everything one would need; clothes, shoes, coats, food and CARE packages by the arm full.

Yes, we experienced the genuine generosity of America.

When people overseas complain about the loud-behaved Americans, I tell them: "Come to America and learn from their Big-Wide Heart."

Maria von Trapp

Stowe, VT

58
Dagmar Havlová
First lady of the Czech Republic; actor

I believe in the sun even though it does not shine,
I believe in God even though he is silent,
I believe in love even though it is concealed.

———————————

Dagmar Havlová is a popular Czech actor of theater, film, and television, and has made over fifty film and two hundred television appearances. She married Czech president Vaclav Havel, and together they have made an indelible impression on the lives of their countrymen—he as a writer, freedom fighter, and president, and she as a tireless leader in support of issues such as environment, education, cancer treatment and prevention, human rights, needs of the handicapped, and racial tolerance.

Dagmar Havlová

I believe in sun even though it does not shine,

I believe in God even though he is silent,

I believe in love even though it is concealed.

59
SIDNEY SHELDON
Writer

Do not judge strangers harshly. Remember that every stranger you meet is you.

Sidney Sheldon won an Academy Award for best original screenplay in 1948 for *The Bachelor and the Bobby-Soxer*, and a Tony Award for the musical *Redhead.* Turning to television, he received several Emmy nominations. Then in 1970, Sheldon released his first novel, *The Naked Face,* won an award for best first mystery novel, and launched a writing career that has made him *Guinness Book of World Records'* most translated author in the world.

Do not judge
strangers harshly.
Remember that
every stranger you
meet is you.

Sidney Sheldon

60
JOAN BROWN CAMPBELL
General Secretary, National Council of Churches

The Bible speaks of love for all as the "more excellent way." We must excel in compassion and reconciliation if we are to make a dangerous and divided world into a place where all can develop their God given gifts.

Reverend Doctor Joan Brown Campbell served as the general secretary of the National Council of Churches of Christ from 1991 to 1998. She has been a leading force in creating opportunities for cooperation among all churches, faiths, and related organizations. She has been an outspoken public speaker and preacher on such topics as racism, women's rights, poverty, and Christian unity.

National Council of the Churches of Christ in the USA

Office of the
General Secretary

The Bible speaks of love for all as the
"more excellent way" We must excel in
compassion and reconciliation if we are
To make a dangerous and divided world
into a place where all can develop their
God given gifts

Rev. Dr. Joan Brown Campbell
General Secretary
National Council of Churches of
Christ in USA.

61

RABBI YECHIEL ECKSTEIN

Religious leader; founder and president, International Fellowship of Christians and Jews

Our search for God in this highly complex and fast-paced, technological world is, in fact, the search for our own selves. His presence can be found in the still, small voices of renewal and hope that surround us all the time, and lead us out from despair—the birth of a child, the buds of a tree in springtime, the wise council of our elders . . . And we are to love God, and continue to believe in the possibility of the world's redemption—and strive to bring it about—"with all our heart, with all our soul and with all our might."

In 1980, when a prominent Christian clergyman declared from the pulpit that God did not hear the prayers of Jews, Jewish people across the country responded with outrage. The less predictable Rabbi Yechiel Z. Eckstein initiated a dialogue with the Christian leader. Eckstein, founder and president of the International Fellowship of Christians and Jews, has set an extraordinary example for leading with understanding, tolerance, and acceptance across cultural and religious divides.

INTERNATIONAL FELLOWSHIP OF CHRISTIANS AND JEWS

RABBI YECHIEL ECKSTEIN
Founder and President

Our search for God in this highly complex & fast-paced, technological world is, in fact, the search for our own selves. His presence can be found in the still, small voices of renewal & hope that surround us all the time, & lead us out from despair — the birth of a child, the buds of a true in springtime, the wise counsel of our elders...

And we are to love God & continue to believe in the possibility of the world's redemption — & strive to bring it about — "with all our heart, with all our soul & with all our might."

Yechiel Eckstein

62
CORAZON C. AQUINO
President of the Philippines

The higher the office, the greater the power, the more one should pray.

Born in 1933 in Tarlac Province in the Philippines, Corazon Aquino married politician Benigno S. Aquino, who was the chief political opponent of Philippine leader Ferdinand Marcos until Aquino was assassinated by a military guard at the Manila airport in 1983. Corazon Aquino took up her husband's cause, leading a nonviolent "people's power" campaign, and won the election to replace Marcos as president. She survived several coup attempts during her presidency (1986–1992) and remains a strong voice for peaceful democratic activism.

CORAZON C. AQUINO

The higher the office, the greater the power,
the more one should pray.

Corazon C. Aquino

Philippines

63
PETER J. GOMES
Minister, The Memorial Church, Harvard University

> One foot in front of the other on the way from where you are to where you are meant to be.

Time magazine named the Reverend Peter J. Gomes one of the seven best preachers in America. His understanding, compassion, grace, and eloquence have bolstered his role as minister to the Harvard University community and as an extraordinary voice for peace and caring around the globe.

One foot in front of the other
on the way from where you are
to where you are
meant to be.

Peter I. Price

64
Barbara Harris
Editor-in-chief, Shape *magazine*

Honor yourself, the truth of who you are. In so doing,
develop yourself fully mind, body and spirit. Always offer
your service without measure. It will fill you up.

Barbara Harris is an expert in the fitness field and has served on a
national level to promote fitness in America's young people. Harris is
a successful publisher and an avid climber as well, having scaled
high peaks around the world.

Honor yourself, the truth
of who you are. In so
doing, develop yourself fully
mind, body and spirit. Always
Offer your service without
measure. It will fill you up.

Barb Harris

ALFRED CORN
Writer; poet

Wherever charity and love are found, so is God.

Alfred Corn III studied at Emory University and Columbia University and earned critical acclaim for his first volume of verse, *All Roads at Once* (1976). His writing illustrates his strong belief in the acceptance of all people, the importance of helping others in need, and the overriding faith he has that God will guide all people to a loving and peaceful place.

ALFRED CORN

" *Ubi caritas et amor, Deus ibi est.* "

66
LAILA ALI
Professional athlete

> Make all of your decisions with good, honest intentions and God will guide you in the right direction. He/She is the best of planners.

————————————

With her famous father watching, Laila Ali made quick work of her first boxing match, knocking out her opponent in sixty-eight seconds. Ali is undefeated (record 10–0, 8 by KO) since her debut in October 1999. She is an inspiration to young women around the world, breaking into a predominantly male sport with dignity, grace, dedication, and success.

Laila Ali

Make all of your decisions with good, honest intentions and God will guide you in the right direction. He/she is the best of planners. *Laila Ali*

67
ZLATA FILIPOVIĆ
Peace advocate; author, Zlata's Diary: A Child's Life in Sarajevo

> Kindness to one another is where the process of building
> peace starts. It takes thoughtfulness and little imagination
> to put yourself in somebody else's shoes. Being so simple,
> why does it not happen more often??

―――――――――

As fighting raged around her in Sarajevo, Zlata Filipović, twelve years old, kept a diary of the horrors of war. The book she wrote during the war in Bosnia, *Zlata's Diary*, was published in 1993. Since then, she has spoken to many schools, universities, and other groups about her experiences and the impact of war on children. A recipient of many awards and honors for her work, Filipović continues to share a story urging peace and understanding. She studied at St. John's College, Oxford University, and continues to be a source of inspiration as her life and work unfold.

Kindness to one another is where the process of building peace starts. It takes thoughtfulness and imagination to put yourself in somebody else's shoes.

Being so simple, why does it not happen more often??

Zlata Filipović

CHAPTER THREE

Teaching

68
NIKKI GIOVANNI
Writer

The most important thing I know about teaching is that the teacher is also learning. Don't think you have to know it all.

———————————

Nikki Giovanni is one of the best-known poets and writers in modern America. She became a leader in the Black Arts Movement, a loose coalition of African American intellectuals who wrote politically and artistically radical poems aimed at raising awareness of black rights and race equality. Her writing has also offered inspirations from her family and her experiences as a single mother.

NIKKI GIOVANNI

The most important thing I know about teaching is that the teacher is also learning. Don't think you have to know it all.

M Giovanni

69
CHARLES MACLAUGHLIN
Teacher

> 36 years ago I was convinced that what and how much I
> knew was most important. . . . Now, in my last year I know
> that love and respect for my students is most important.
> The other day, Erica, one of my current students, said, "Mr.
> Mac, you should write about truth and trust . . . that's you."
> I'm glad I am a teacher.

Charles MacLaughlin, or "Mr. Mac," as his students refer to him, is
the founder of the Heritage Program at Quincy High School in
Massachusetts. MacLaughlin designed the program to provide an
alternative learning approach and made headlines for the successes
it achieved with students like Lauralee Summer, who was at risk of
not graduating from high school, but, through Mr. Mac's program,
was accepted at Harvard University and graduated in 1999.

Quincy High Schools
Tech Prep Team

Explore
Experience
Understand
Connect

Charles MacLaughlin

the most important thing I Know...
About Teaching

36 years ago I was convinced that
what & how much I Knew was most
important....

Now, in my last year I Know that
love & respect for my students is most
important. The other day Ereca, one of
my current students said "MR. Mac
you should write about Truth & Trust
... That's you." I'm glad I am a
Teacher

Mr. Mac

70
NORMAN CONARD
Teacher; USA Today's All-USA Teacher First Team winner, 2000–2001.

A student who changes one person, changes the world . . .
thus the power of one.

Norm Conard teaches tolerance and diversity in an overwhelmingly white, rural school in Uniontown, Kansas, by having students research multicultural history projects. His social studies and video production classes created a student film on integration that led to the reunion of Elizabeth Eckford, one of the Little Rock Nine integration pioneers, and Ken Reinhardt, a white student who befriended her at the time, in an event that was covered nationally by CNN News.

Uniontown High School

A student who changes
one person, changes
the world....... thus
the power of one.

Mom Conrad

71
KENNETH R. BAIN
Teaching scholar, Searle Center for Teaching Excellence, Northwestern University

Teaching should be thought of as helping and encouraging other people to learn. People learn most deeply (in ways that have a sustained, substantial, and positive influence on the way they think, act, interact, or feel) when they are trying to solve problems or answer questions that they regard as interesting, important, or beautiful.

———

Kenneth R. Bain is founding director of the Searle Center for Teaching Excellence and a faculty member at Northwestern University. Internationally recognized for his insights into teaching and learning and for a twelve-year study on best teaching practices, he has presented teaching workshops at more than three dozen universities around the world. He has received numerous teaching awards from the Harry S. Truman Library, Lyndon Baines Johnson Library, the Ford Foundation, the National Endowment for the Humanities, and the International Studies Association, among others.

Teaching should be thought of as helping and encouraging other people to learn. People learn most deeply (in ways that have a sustained, substantial and positive influence on the way they think, act, interact, or feel) when they are trying to solve problems or answer questions that they regard as interesting, important, or beautiful.

Kenneth R. Bain

72

KAREN ZUMWALT
Educator, Columbia University Teachers College

When you stop learning from your teaching, you should stop teaching.

––––––––––

Karen Zumwalt is professor of education at the Columbia University Teachers College. Her focus is instilling in its students the capability to solve problems, motivate learners, inspire hope, raise standards, and take charge of change. It is an approach that leads our students, the future teachers of our children, to value independent thinking and persist in lifelong learning.

When you stop learning
from your teaching,
you should stop
teaching.

Karen Zumwalt

73
Lenny Wilkens
Basketball coach, winningest in NBA history

Teachers impact our lives, by opening the doors to the
world through education. Education allows us to have a say
about what we do and what we become. They help us see
that life is a challenge we must accept.

The winningest coach in National Basketball Association history
recently began as the new head coach of the Toronto Raptors. He is
one of only two people in history to be acknowledged in the
Basketball Hall of Fame as both player and coach.

TORONTO RAPTORS BASKETBALL CLUB

Teachers impact our lives, by opening
the doors to the World Through Education.
Education allows us to have a say about
what we do and what we become. They
help us see that Life is a challenge we
must accept.

Lenny Wilkens

74
JAMES M. MONTEBELL
Teacher; Junior Achievement's 2000 National Teacher of the Year

Being a teacher for the past 35 years, one thing I try not to ever forget . . . don't give up on a student. Just when you think all is lost, they might begin to respond and achieve personal and academic success. Their self-esteem will grow and flourish.

The Junior Achievement Teacher of the Year Award is bestowed upon a high school educator who goes above and beyond to teach students to understand economics, business, and free enterprise using Junior Achievement high school programs. Montebell used the Junior Achievement model for over two decades, and actively involves his students in community projects and writing articles about their work.

Thomas McKean High School

James M. Montebell
Social Studies Chairperson

Being a teacher for the past 35 years, one thing I try not to ever forget... don't give up on a student. Just when you think all is lost, they might begin to respond and achieve personal and academic success. Their self-esteem will grow and flourish.

James M. Montebell

75
Marie Myung-Ok Lee
Writer; professor at Yale

I have found that in teaching, as in life, it helps to be prepared.

Marie Lee's first novel, *Finding My Voice,* won the Friends of American Writers Award and widespread critical acclaim. She is a founder of the Asian American Writers' Workshop, which has become the premiere resource for writers, readers, and publishers of literature written by Asians living in America, and one of the most active community-based arts organizations in the United States.

Marie Myung-Ok Lee

I have found that in teaching, as
in life, it helps to be prepared.

Marie Lee

76

MARGE CHRISTENSEN GOULD
Teacher; USA Today's All-USA Teacher First Team winner,
2000–2001.

It is the combination of high-tech/high touch/high
expectations that makes the real difference for students,
especially at-risk students, and improves their chances of
success in school and in the real world.

———————————

Marge Gould has been teaching for twenty-six years. Her motto,
"high-tech, high touch, high expectation" defines her one-to-one stu-
dent-to-teacher interaction principle, and her commitment to having
each student reach his or her potential, and not just "get by." She
makes her students responsible for their own progress in a self-
paced program emphasizing reading, writing, computer skills, and job
marketability.

Marge Christensen Gould
All USA Teacher Team 2000

It is the combination of high-tech/high level/high expectations that makes the real difference for students, especially at-risk students, and improves their chances of success in school and in the real world.

Marge Christensen Gould

77
Roger Schank, Ph.D.
Educator; founder of Cognitive Arts

> Learning is an emotional experience. Failure enhances the experience. You can't learn by being told. School is, for the most part, a waste of time. Educators who are concerned with assessment are not concerned with learning. Learning and schooling have next to nothing in common. If you want to learn, go out and experience something.

Roger C. Schank is a leader in the field of artificial intelligence and multimedia-based interactive training. His work stresses the powerful benefits of experiential learning realized through learning from experts, encouraging students to make mistakes and developing skills rather than perfecting routines.

Cognitive**Arts**

Learning is an emotional experience. Failure enhances the experience. You can't learn by being told. School is, for the most part, a waste of time. Educators who are concerned with assessment are not concerned with learning. Learning and schooling have next to nothing in common. If you want to learn, go out and experience something.

Roger Schank

78
Margaret C. Collier
Teacher; USA Today's All-USA Teacher First Team winner, 2000–2001

> When you enrich the mind of a child, you open another window to the wonders of our world.

Teamed for two years to teach the bottom quarter of the class at the Millennium Middle School in Sanford, Florida, Margaret Collier and Mary Cook found a way to boost self-esteem and academic skills in their students while creating a joy for learning in them. The two created the award-winning TIERS (Teaching Integrated Education Through Related Subject Areas) curriculum; their art-infused classes are often directed by students and include music, painting, sculpture, and hands-on learning.

MARGARET C. COLLIER

When you enrich the
mind of a child, you
open another window
to the wonders of our world.

79
MARY T. COOK
Teacher; USA Today's *All-USA Teacher First Team winner,*
2000–2001

> No carefully crafted lesson or extended years of study will
> educate a child as thoroughly as an encouraging word, a
> gentle squeeze to the shoulder or a shared laugh. Your
> students may not remember what you taught them but they
> will remember how you treated them.

Teamed for two years to teach the bottom quarter of the class at the
Millennium Middle School in Sanford, Florida, Mary Cook and
Margaret Collier found a way to boost self-esteem and academic
skills in their students while creating a joy for learning in them. The
two created the award-winning TIERS (Teaching Integrated Education
Through Related Subject Areas) curriculum; their art-infused classes
are often directed by students and include music, painting, sculpture,
and hands-on learning.

**Millennium Middle School
Fine Arts, Communication
and Pre-International
Baccalaureate Magnet**

No carefully crafted lesson or extended years of study will educate a child as thoroughly as an encouraging word, a gentle squeeze to the shoulder or a shared laugh.

Your students may not remember what you taught them but they will remember how you treated them.

Mary T. (Terry) Cook

SEMINOLE COUNTY
PUBLIC SCHOOLS

80
MICHAEL S. COMEAU
*Teacher; USA Today's All-USA Teacher First Team winner,
2000–2001*

> To teach is to make a difference in a child's life every
> minute of every day . . . long after they have left the
> classroom.

As a fourth-grade teacher, Michael Comeau expects 120 percent of
every student every day, and gives at least that much of himself. The
Waller Elementary School serves as an English-as-a-second-
language hub and draws students from impoverished neighborhoods.
Comeau finds that teaching with hands-on projects, using textbooks as
a reference source, has been the secret to his students' inspiration.

To TEACH IS TO MAKE A DIFFERENCE
IN A CHILD'S LIFE EVERY MINUTE OF
EVERY DAY ... LONG AFTER THEY HAVE LEFT
YOUR CLASSROOM.

MICHAEL S. COMEAU
4TH GRADE TEACHER

81
Lisa J. Arnold
Teacher; USA Today's All-USA Teacher First Team winner, 2000–2001

Teaching is caring. Learning knows no bounds for a student who knows that his teacher cares. Good teachers care enough to "walk in students' shoes" to know them better. Great teachers know that, in order to "walk in someone else's shoes," you must first take off your own shoes.

———

At the Riverview Elementary School in Sioux City, Iowa, Lisa Arnold teaches her students that music is the universal language, and through music, she teaches them multicultural appreciation. Arnold formed the Multicultural Musical Instrument Factory, in which students make instruments from cultures they study, and also initiated Project Worldsong, a national partnership of elementary schools to share writings, photos, and tapes of multicultural music from their areas. She successfully engages her students in the love of music, the love and appreciation of other cultures, and the acceptance of all cultures as having something unique to share.

A Rainbow of Cultures

Lisa J. Arnold, Music Specialist

Teaching is caring. Learning knows no bounds for a student who knows that his teacher cares. Good teachers care enough to "walk in students' shoes" to know them better. Great teachers know that, in order to "walk in someone else's shoes," you must first take off your own shoes.

Lisa J. Arnold

82
KALI KURDY
Teacher; Nasdaq Teacher of the Year, 2000

> Good teachers inspire students to have confidence in them.
> Great teachers inspire students to have confidence in
> themselves.

As the First Grand Winner of Nasdaq National Teaching Awards, Kali Kurdy was recognized for excellence in economics education. Kurdy's teaching is helping to prepare America's youth to become wise consumers, knowledgeable investors, productive members of the workforce, and active community participants. These are lessons that the students will take far away from their economics classrooms and into the future as leaders and active citizens in communities around the country and around the world.

Good teachers inspire
students to have confidence
in them.

Great teachers inspire
students to have
confidence in themselves.

Kali Kurdy

CHAPTER FOUR

Success and Excellence

83
TED TURNER
Business leader; entrepreneur; sailor; philanthropist

How much you give is how you keep score.

Founder of CNN, winner of the America's Cup, owner of some of the nation's most successful sports teams, founder of the Goodwill Games, and one of the nation's leading philanthropists, Ted Turner is one of the most influential and creative leaders of the late twentieth and early twenty-first centuries.

TIME WARNER

R.E. Turner
Vice Chairman

How much you give is how you keep score.

Ted Turner

84
CONDOLEEZZA RICE
International affairs scholar; national security adviser to President George W. Bush

> Excellence is born of having higher expectations of yourself than anyone could possibly have of you.

———

Condoleezza Rice became the first woman of African American heritage to be named to a Cabinet position, serving as national security adviser to President George W. Bush. Prior to this appointment, Rice was on the faculty at Stanford University and held the post of provost from 1992 to 1999.

Excellence is born of having higher expectations of yourself than anyone could possibly have of you.

Condoleezza Rice

85
PATRICK RAFTER
Athlete; tennis champion

> You come into this world with nothing and you leave with
> nothing. Live life to the fullest.

———————

Patrick Rafter is recognized as a superb ambassador for tennis and
for Australia. He is the recipient of sportsmanship and humanitarian
awards worldwide, all while being ranked number one in the world in
1999, and in the top ten for five years. He founded the Patrick Rafter
Cherish the Children Foundation, inspired by his personal desire to
help homeless children, children who suffer physical and or emotional disabilities, victims of abuse, and others, in order to give them
the hope and the care they need.

You come Into this world with nothing
and you leave with nothing
Live life to the fullest.

86
MUHAMMAD ALI
Professional athlete

> The most important thing I know about the spirit of sport is that one has to be fit in both body and mind. Whether it's boxing, basketball, or badminton, one must be ready to succeed before entering the arena . . . long before the lights come up.

———————

Forty years after winning the gold medal at the 1960 Rome Olympics and after capturing the world heavyweight championship three times, Muhammad Ali remains a revered sports figure and supporter of charities across the country and around the world. Ali brought unparalleled speed and grace to his sport, while his charm and wit changed the image of a boxing champion. Ali has received countless honors and awards for his work outside the ring as well, most recently the "Messenger of Peace," presented to him by United Nations Secretary General Kofi Annan for his efforts feeding the hungry around the globe.

GREATEST OF ALL TIME, INC.

The most important thing I know about the spirit of sport is that one has to be fit in both body and mind. Whether it's boxing, basketball, or badminton, one must be ready to succeed before entering the arena... long before the lights come up.

Muhammad Ali

87
DAVID PACKARD
Business leader; inventor; cofounder of Hewlett-Packard

The way to win, whatever the game: Get the best players, develop a spirit of teamwork and get them all fired up with a will to win.

With his college friend William Hewlett, David Packard launched their company in 1939 in a garage and built a company that has led technological advances for over fifty years. He believed in a close relationship between management and employees and often just walked the halls of his buildings talking with and learning from his employees. When Packard died in 1996, he left the bulk of his estate to the Packard Foundation, making it one of the largest private foundations in the world, with a $9 billion endowment.

The Way to win, whatever
the game
Get the best players, Develop
a spirit of teamwork
and Get them all fined
up with a
Will to Win

David Packard

88
SHEILA E. WIDNALL, PH.D.
Secretary of the Air Force

The Air Force has chosen "excellence in all you do" as one of our core values. We have found that a commitment to excellence is central not just to doing our work well but to finding all the joy there is in life. If you don't push yourself toward excellence you're cheating yourself. Treat yourself right—push yourself hard!

Sheila E. Widnall, Ph.D., served as secretary of the Air Force, the only woman ever to head a branch of the U.S. military. Master pilot, astrophysicist, aeronautical genius, lauded educator, prolific writer, and compassionate human being are the phrases used to describe this extraordinary woman. She received the 1998 Living Legacy Award from the Women's International Center for her career accomplishments.

THE SECRETARY OF THE AIR FORCE
WASHINGTON

The Air Force has chosen "excellence in all you do" as one of our core values. We have found that a commitment to excellence is central not just to doing our work well but to finding all the joy there is in life. If you don't push yourself toward excellence ~~you cheat yourself~~ ..., treat yourself right — push yourself hard!

[signature]

89
ROBERT BALLARD
Oceanographer

Follow your dream!

Robert Ballard, scientist, educator, author, and hands-on explorer, may have the highest public profile of any scientist alive today, having found the wreck of the *Titanic* in 1985, followed by finding several other famous lost ships of the twentieth century: the *Lusitania,* the *Bismarck,* and the *Yorktown*. Each year, with his JASON Project, Ballard takes six hundred to seven hundred thousand children on underwater explorations via live satellite video, inspiring many children with a love of science.

INSTITUTE FOR EXPLORATION

Follow your dream!

90
TERRY ORLICK, PH.D.
Author, In Pursuit of Excellence

Excellence is a combination of passion and focus. When you have passion for what you are doing and get your focus in the right place, everything else will follow. Embrace the moment.

Terry Orlick is a renowned educator and internationally recognized leader in the field of performance enhancement and has worked with thousands of Olympic and professional athletes, coaches, business leaders, astronauts, and others to help them realize their potential in sport, work, and life. Orlick is the author of more than two hundred articles and twenty-four books, which have sold over a million copies worldwide, including the highly acclaimed *In Pursuit of Excellence.*

Excellence is a combination of passion and Focus. When you have passion for what you are doing and get your focus in the right place, everything else will follow.
Embrace The moment.

Terry Orlick

91
DORIAN YATES
Mr. Olympia, five-time winner

> If you strive to exceed yourself and be the very best you can,
> you will always be a winner.

When he was a teenager, Dorian Yates got himself into trouble. He
served six months at Whatton Youth Detention Centre, where he
earned a reputation as the strongest of the three hundred inmates
and developed a new self-respect. He has since won five Mr. Olympia
titles and is an example to young people that they have a choice
about the outcome of their lives.

DORIAN YATES - MR. OLYMPIA

IF YOU STRIVE TO EXCEED YOURSELF
AND BE THE VERY BEST YOU
CAN, YOU WILL ALWAYS BE
A WINNER.

92

PAUL SIMON
U.S. *senator*

> Excellence should not be a quality that a limited elite strive
> for and possess, but a quality that everyone should have an
> opportunity to achieve.

A U.S. senator from Illinois from 1985 to 1997, Paul Simon gained a reputation for his conservative fiscal policies. At age nineteen, he bought a small-town newspaper in Troy, New York, and earned a reputation as a crusader against political corruption. He is the author of more than a dozen books on politics and history.

United States Senate
WASHINGTON, DC 20510-1302

Excellence should not be a
quality that a limited
elite strive for and possess,
but a quality that everyone
should have an opportunity
to achieve —

Paul Simon

93
CHRISTINE TODD WHITMAN
Governor of New Jersey; director of EPA for President George W. Bush

Anything worth doing is worth doing well.

Christine Todd Whitman, a moderate Republican, became New Jersey's first female governor in 1994, winning on a platform of tax reform and women's reproductive rights. In 2001, President George W. Bush named Whitman to head the Environmental Protection Agency (EPA), and declared that the EPA would, for the first time, become a Cabinet-level appointment.

Anything worth doing is
worth doing well.

Christie Whitman

94

CLIFF MEIDL
Olympic athlete

> Maximize yourself as an individual. Use your strengths,
> determination and dreams and be the best that you can be.
> Success and happiness is determined by one's own
> achievements.

———————

Cliff Meidl was a twenty-year-old construction worker in California when he cut into a power line and electrocuted himself. Thirty thousand volts of electricity coursed through his body at that moment, fifteen times the power of the electric chair. And yet, Meidl was revived, overcame the debilitating effects of the injury, took up kayaking to aid his rehabilitation, and ultimately earned a spot on the U.S. Olympic kayaking team and led the entire U.S. delegation into the 2000 Summer Olympics as a symbol of the triumph of the human spirit.

Maximize yourself as an individual. Use your strengths, determination and dreams and be the best that you can be. Success and happiness is determined by one's own achievements.

Cliff Meidl

95
Pat Williams
Sports leader; Orlando Magic team president and CEO

Walt Disney had an outline on excellence that has had an enormous impact on me: 1. Think tomorrow—make today an investment in tomorrow. 2. Free up your imagination— we can usually do more than we ever thought we could. 3. Strive for lasting quality—don't cut corners, do everything the best you can the first time. 4. Stick-to-it- ivity—don't quit too soon; hang in there. 5. Have fun!

***

Pat Williams is widely recognized in the sports world as a great leader and manager, but perhaps is best known today as a premiere motivational speaker. Williams has also authored a number of moti- vational books offering inspiration to his readers. In 1996, Williams was named one of the fifty most influential people in NBA history, exemplifying the benefits of hard work, imagination, determination, and excellence.

THOUGHTS ON EXCELLENCE

WALT DISNEY HAD AN OUTLINE ON EXCELLENCE THAT HAS HAD AN ENORMOUS IMPACT ON ME.

1. THINK TOMORROW — (MAKE TODAY AN INVESTMENT IN TOMORROW)

2. FREE UP YOUR IMAGINATION (WE CAN USUALLY DO MORE THAN WE EVER THOUGHT WE COULD.)

3. STRIVE FOR LASTING QUALITY (DON'T CUT CORNERS; DO EVERYTHING THE BEST YOU CAN THE FIRST TIME.)

4. STICK-TO-IT-IVITY (DON'T QUIT TOO SOON; HANG IN THERE.)

5 HAVE FUN!

96
Dr. Henry C. Lee
Forensic pathologist; key witness in the O. J. Simpson trial

The winner is always part of the answer; the loser always is part of the problem. The winner always has a program; the loser always has an excuse. The winner says let me do it for you; the loser says that's not my job. The winner says it may be difficult but it's possible; the loser says it may be possible, but it's too difficult. Be a winner.

Henry Lee is widely considered to be one of the most skilled forensic scientists in the world. Lee has participated in the investigation of more than five thousand cases over the course of his career. He also has provided global leadership in applying forensic science to unravel abuses of human rights in pursuit of truth and justice.

State of Connecticut

DEPARTMENT OF PUBLIC SAFETY

Dr. Henry C. Lee
Commissioner

The winner is always part of the answer:
the loser always is part of the problem.

The winner always has a program:
the loser always has an excuse.

The winner says let me do it for you:
the loser says that's not my job.

The winner says it may be difficult but it's possible:
the loser says it may be possible, but it too difficult

Be a Winner

Henry Lee

97
LEONARD KLEINROCK, PH.D.
Scientist; Internet innovator

Great success is within your grasp if you set your sights high
enough. Life is too short and too precious to settle for
mediocrity. But take care never to sacrifice your honor,
trust, compassion, or self-esteem in your pursuits.

Leonard Kleinrock is credited with creating packet switching, the
technology underpinning the Internet, while he was a graduate student at MIT. This discovery came a full decade before what is widely
considered the "birth of the Internet," which occurred when his host
computer at UCLA became the first node of the Internet in September
1969. Additionally, Kleinrock has launched the field of nomadic com-
puting, an emerging mobile technology to support computer and communication needs as people travel from place to place.

LEONARD KLEINROCK, Ph.D.

Great success is within your
grasp if you set your sights
high enough. Life is too short &
too precious to settle for mediocrity.
But take care never to sacrifice
your honor, trust, compassion or
self esteem in your pursuits.

Leonard Kleinrock

98
SHANNON HENRY
Writer; reporter, Washington Post

> Be yourself! Imagine how boring the world would be if we
> were all exactly the same.

Known as the "dot-com diva," Shannon Henry has a reputation as
one of the nation's leading technology writers. *Washington Business
Forward* magazine named her one of the Top 40 Agenda Setters and
Market Movers in the capital.

Shannon Henry

Be yourself! Imagine how boring the world would be if we were all exactly the same.

Shannon Henry

99
Metropolitan Iakovos
Religious leader; archbishop of the Greek Orthodox Church, Chicago

> Glory to God in the highest! This is the only sure way to
> excellence.

Metropolitan Iakovos is bishop of Chicago in the Greek Orthodox
Church. His dedication to helping young people overcome hurdles
and reach for excellence not only through determination, but also by
strengthening their faith in themselves and others, is improving communities throughout the United States.

Glory to God in The highest!
This is the only sure way
to Excellence.

Archbishop Iakovos.

100

AGNES GUND
President, Museum of Modern Art

> Excellence is working as hard as possible on something
> about which you care deeply; at the end of which you
> should be able to say that you have achieved all that is
> possible.

Agnes Gund has served as president of the Museum of Modern Art since 1991. In 1977, she founded the Studio in a School Association, an organization that places professional artists in public schools to educate children about art, of which she remains an active trustee. She is the recipient of numerous awards, including the National Medal of the Arts, presented by the president of the United States.

Agnes Gund
President

Excellence is working as hard as possible on something about which you care deeply; at the end of which you should be able to say that you have achieved all that is possible.

Agnes Gund

101
John H. Chafee
U.S. senator

Nothing beats an early start.

Born in 1922 in Providence, Rhode Island, John Chafee was a graduate of Yale University and Harvard Law School and had an illustrious political and community service career until his death in 1999. Chafee served as governor of Rhode Island, secretary of the Navy, and U.S. senator. He was known for his nonpartisan advocacy for education and women's rights, and was widely admired as a thoughtful and fair statesman.

" Nothing beats an early start"

John H. Chafee

102

ARLENE BLUM
Explorer; writer; motivational speaker

I try to act in accord with the Buddhist precept of
increasing the happiness and decreasing the suffering of all
living creatures.

———————————

Arlene Blum has played a leading role in more than fifteen successful
mountaineering expeditions, including climbs of Mount Everest and
Mount McKinley. She is the author of *Annapurna: A Woman's Place*,
has a doctorate in biophysical chemistry, and has taught at Stanford
University, Wellesley College, and U.C. Berkeley. Blum has won a gold
medal from the Society of Women Geographers, an honor previously
awarded to the likes of Amelia Earhart, Margaret Mead, and Mary
Leakey.

Arlene Blum
LECTURES

I try to act in accord with the Buddhist precept of increasing the happiness & decreasing the suffering of all living creatures

Arlene Blum

arlene@arleneblum.com
Web: www.arleneblum.com

103

Ernest F. Hollings
U.S. senator

> To achieve excellence, you must focus, work hard and
> persevere.

———————————

At age thirty-six, Fritz Hollings was elected the youngest governor in
the history of his state. He went on to be elected to the U.S. Senate
and has become widely admired for his character and leadership on
challenging issues. He believes that performance is better than
promise and he has modeled his career of public service under that
creed—a lifetime spent working to provide economic opportunity to
everyone and to make government fiscally accountable to the people.

United States Senate

WASHINGTON, D. C. 20510

To achieve excellence, you must focus,
work hard and persevere.

Best of luck in your efforts,

Fritz Hollings

104
JACK LEMMON
Actor; Academy Award winner, Best Actor, 1955 and 1973

Anything truly worthwhile does not come easy. (If it did, it would not be all that worthwhile.)

Jack Lemmon was born in Boston, Massachusetts, studied at Harvard, served in the Navy, and was a singing waiter before breaking out as a film and stage actor. *Some Like It Hot* spiked his career, and he continued with Oscar-winning performances for *Mister Roberts* (1955) and *Save the Tiger* (1973). Lemmon received the American Film Institute Life Achievement Award in 1988 and was one of the most widely respected and admired stars in the business.

Anything truly worthwhile does not come easy.
(If it did, it would not be all that worthwhile.)

Jack Lemmon

DR. BARUJ BENACERRAF
Winner of the Nobel Prize in physiology or medicine, 1980

To achieve excellence, I found that I needed to always examine my own work with a merciless critical eye. It is far better to be more severe and demanding of oneself than others can be. Accordingly, since nature is far more complex and unpredictable than we can ever expect, I have learned most from my own shortcomings than from any other source.

An immunologist, born in Caracas, Venezuela, in 1920, Baruj Benacerraf shared the 1980 Nobel Prize for his contributions to the discovery of immune-response genes that regulate immunology in organ transplants. His work continues to help thousands of people who suffer from various forms of cancer and offers hope that a cure for cancer will one day be discovered.

Dr. Baruj Benacerraf

Per aspera ad astra!
To achieve excellence, I found that I
needed to always examine my own work
with a merciless critical eye. It is far
better to be more severe and demanding of
oneself than others can be.

Accordingly, since Nature is far more complex
and unpredictable than we can ever expect,
I have learned most from my own
shortcomings than from any other source.

Baruj Benacerraf

EDWARD O. WITTEN
Physicist, Institute for Advanced Study, Princeton

The most interesting and important goals often look out of reach until you've reached them!

A physicist and mathematician, Edward Witten became professor of physics at Princeton University in 1980, then professor of natural sciences at the Institute for Advanced Study in 1987. A central figure in the study of superstrings, he has made many important contributions to theoretical physics.

The most interesting
and important goals
often look out of
reach until you've
reached them!

Edward Witten

WILLIAM N. LIPSCOMB
Winner of the Nobel Prize in chemistry, 1976

Unusual achievement in science comes to those who risk failure, and often criticism, in the pursuit of new or undeveloped ideas: ideas which have the potential to change science itself. Extensive and detailed knowledge, and choice of significant research are equally important, as are excellent colleagues and teachers.

Under the influence of Linus Pauling at California Institute of Technology, Lipscomb learned to love the science of chemistry. He joined the faculty at Harvard University, where his groundbreaking work led to his being awarded the Nobel Prize in chemistry for study of the structure and bonding of boron compounds and the general nature of chemical bonding.

Unusual achievement in science comes to those who risk failure, and often criticism, in the pursuit of new or undeveloped ideas: ideas which have the potential to change science itself. Extensive and detailed knowledge, and choice of significant research are equally important, as are excellent colleagues and teachers.

William N. Lipscomb

108
PAUL BERG
Winner of the Nobel Prize in chemistry, 1980

The most important thing is not to let your talents and learning be wasted. Aim high, try hard, don't let adversity or skepticism deflect you from your goals; above all, don't lose your enthusiasm and idealism, and keep a sense of humor and enjoy life.

Paul Berg was born in New York City in 1926 and spent much of his career on the faculty of Stanford University. His pioneering experiments with recombinant DNA have resulted in the development of new technologies of genetic engineering that may one day cure diseases such as cancer and AIDS.

ARNOLD AND MABEL BECKMAN CENTER
FOR MOLECULAR AND GENETIC MEDICINE
Paul Berg, Director

Cahill Professor in Cancer Research
Department of Biochemistry

The most important thing is not to let your talents and learning be wasted. Aim high, try hard, don't let adversity or skepticism deflect you from your goals; above all, don't lose your enthusiasm and idealism, and keep a sense of humor and enjoy life.

Paul Berg
Nobel laureate, Chemistry 1980

109
DANIEL J. BOORSTIN
Winner of the Pulitzer Prize in history, 1974

> The great obstacle to progress is not ignorance but the
> illusion of knowledge. The best antidote to that illusion is
> to prepare for the unexpected.

———————

A historian educated at Harvard, Oxford, and Yale Universities, Daniel Boorstin taught at the University of Chicago, went on to become the director of the National Museum of Natural History, and librarian of the Library of Congress. His Pulitzer Prize–winning trilogy *The Americans: The Democratic Experience* (1953–1973) reflects his belief that people, experiences, and inventions are far more important than ideology.

The great obstacle to progress
is not ignorance but the
illusion of knowledge. The
best antidote to that illusion
is to prepare for the _unexpected_.

Daniel Boorstin

110

VERNON J. BAKER
Congressional Medal of Honor winner, 1997

> Be yourself, don't try to emulate anyone else. Give yourself
> a goal to accomplish and on the way to self-fulfillment take
> responsibility for your actions.

On January 13, 1997, to correct a record of racial prejudice that lasted more than fifty years, President Bill Clinton awarded seven African American soldiers of World War II our nation's highest military award, the Medal of Honor. Second Lieutenant Vernon J. Baker, then seventy-eight years old, was the only veteran alive to accept his award but did so in a way that honored all those who suffered such prejudice.

Vernon J. Baker

"Be yourself, don't try to
emulate any one else. Give yourself a goal to accomplish & on
the way to self fulfillment take
responsibility for your actions."
I ope this will suffice.
                Thank you
                Vernon J Baker
                    C.M.H.

111

Kim B. Clark
Dean of Harvard Business School

> Wise and inspired words: "No success can compensate for
> failure in the home." "The most important work you will do
> in your life will be done within the walls of your home."

Kim Clark attended Harvard University but left after only a year to become a missionary. He returned to Harvard, earned several degrees, and joined the faculty, where he served for twenty years, focusing on technology, competition, and industry evolution. Clark rose to become dean of the Harvard Business School and has been an inspiring voice urging students to lead not just with extraordinary work skills, but also with a focus on personal mission, values, and character.

HARVARD UNIVERSITY

GRADUATE SCHOOL OF BUSINESS ADMINISTRATION

GEORGE F. BAKER FOUNDATION

KIM B. CLARK
Dean of the Faculty
Harry E. Figgie, Jr. Professor of
 Business Administration

SOLDIERS FIELD
BOSTON, MASSACHUSETTS 02163

Wise and inspired words:

"*No success can compensate
for failure in the home.*"

"*The most important work you
will do in your life will be
done within the walls of your
home.*"

112

CAROL MOSELEY-BRAUN
U.S. senator

A poem my late mother recited many times:

> If a job is once begun
> Never stop until it's done
> Be the job large or small
> Do it right
> Or not at all.

Carol Moseley-Braun was a Democratic senator from Illinois and the first African American woman elected to the U.S. Senate. She was elected to the Senate in 1992 and has since supported a variety of legislative causes, including child care, women in business, and education. Since leaving the Senate, Moseley-Braun has served as ambassador to New Zealand and Samoa.

CAROL MOSELEY-BRAUN
UNITED STATES SENATOR

A Poem my late mother Recited many times:

If a job is once begun
Never stop until its done
Be the job large or small
Do it right
Or not at all —

Carol Moseley Braun

113

RUDOLPH A. MARCUS, PH.D.
Winner of the Nobel Prize in chemistry, 1992

> Be willing to take a leap. It's been my experience that you often have to go onto uncertain ground—it's not easy, but you cover a lot more territory that way and might even, to your surprise, uncover something new.

———————————

Rudy Marcus leads a group of researchers at California Institute of Technology that formulates and investigates theories of chemical reactions. In 1992, Marcus was awarded the Nobel Prize in chemistry for his contributions to the theory of electron transfer reactions in chemical systems. Marcus insists that treading into new territory creates fear, but the uncertainty of experimentation and the striving for excellence is what leads to discoveries that change the world of science.

CALIFORNIA INSTITUTE OF TECHNOLOGY
Division of Chemistry and Chemical Engineering

Rudolph A. Marcus
Arthur Amos Noyes Professor of Chemistry

Be willing to take a leap. It's been
my experience that you often have to go
onto uncertain ground - it's not easy,
but you cover a lot more territory that
way and might even, to your surprise,
uncover something new.

Rudy Marcus

114

JOSEPH E. MURRAY, M.D.
Winner of the Nobel Prize in physiology or medicine, 1990

Always do what is right. Never give up. Never! Curiosity, imagination and persistence are the only requirements for a clinical scientist.

Joseph Murray performed the first human kidney transplant between identical twins in 1954. After investigating the effects of immuno-suppressant drugs, he then performed the first human kidney transplant from an unrelated donor in 1962. For this lifesaving research, Murray shared the 1990 Nobel Prize in medicine. In addition to this pioneering work, he was trained in plastic surgery and worked to correct facial defects in children, improving their looks and their outlooks on the future.

JOSEPH E. MURRAY, M.D. (Emeritus)
PROFESSOR OF SURGERY
CHIEF OF PLASTIC SURGERY:
  Brigham & Women's Hospital
  Children's Hospital

" Always do what's right"

" Never give up. Never!"

" Curiosity, imagination & persistence are the
   only requirements for a clinical scientist."

Joseph E. Murray, M.D.

115

Dr. Benjamin S. Carson Sr., M.D.
Neurological surgeon

> If you need something done, you must ask a busy person to
> do it, because people who are not busy never have time to
> do anything because it takes them all day to do nothing.

————————————

Ben Carson grew up in poverty but with his mother's love, expectations, and encouragement, he realized his dream of becoming a doctor. Carson gained worldwide recognition for his talent in pediatric
surgery, separating twins who were joined at the head. He is
cofounder of the Carson Scholars Fund, which recognizes young people of all backgrounds for exceptional academic and humanitarian
accomplishments, and he has authored several inspiring books.

Neurological Surgery

Benjamin S. Carson, Sr., M.D.
Director, Pediatric Neurosurgery

If you need something done, you must ask a busy person to do it, because people who are not busy never have time to do anything because it takes them all day to do nothing.

Ben Carson

116

Bella Abzug
Feminist leader

> Too many think excellence is hard to attain. Actually to strive for growth and self-expression is within reach of all of us. If we believe in ourselves, we can develop our own standard of excellence and that's what counts.

Bella Abzug was a feminist, a lawyer, and a politician. She was born in New York City and died in 1998. A prominent figure in peace campaigning, she was the founder of Women Strike for Peace in 1961 and the National Women's Political Caucus. She was elected to Congress in 1971 and was one of the most influential women in the feminist movement, responsible for much political and social change for the benefit of women and the poor.

Dear Mr. Adrian —

For many that Excellence is hard to attain. Actually to strive for growth and self-expression is within reach of all of us.

If we believe in ourselves, we can develop our own standard of excellence and that is what counts

Sincerely,

Bella Abzug

117
ROALD HOFFMAN
Winner of the Nobel Prize in chemistry, 1981

Unsatisfied with the adequacy of your own work, but
striving with all the craftsmanship at your command,
speaking through your work to others, you will create . . .
excellence.

Named for Roald Amundsen, Roald Hoffman was born in Poland just
before World War II. His family hid from the Nazis during the war, but
his father was killed for organizing an escape attempt, and most of
his family suffered a similar fate. He came to the United States and
studied at schools in New York, then went on to earn degrees at
Columbia and Harvard. He has taught at Cornell since 1965 and was
awarded the Nobel Prize in chemistry for his studies.

Cornell University

Department of Chemistry
Baker Laboratory

Unsatisfied with the adequacy
of your own work, but striving
with all the craftsmanship at
your command, speaking through
your work to others, you will
create ... excellence

Roald Hoffmann

118

LEROY NEIMAN
Artist

You may be sure that everything you put into your art will give you full return.

─────────────

Leroy Neiman is recognized as the premiere sports artist of the twentieth century. In 1972, Neiman was named the official artist of the Olympic Games and in 1979 was honored with the Olympic Artist of the Century Award. He loves his work and teaching others and hopes that his work inspires others to follow their dreams, and to be happy with whatever endeavor they enter.

You may be sure
that everything
you put into your
art will give
you full return

LeRoy Neiman

LEROY
NEIMAN

119

JULIUS AXELROD
Winner of the Nobel Prize in physiology or medicine, 1970

To achieve excellence in scientific research, one must be highly motivated, exercise good judgment, have imagination, determination, savvy, luck, and the ability to ask the right questions at the right time.

Born in New York City in 1912, Julius Axelrod began his chemistry career at the Laboratory of Industrial Hygiene in New York City from 1935 to 1945. In 1955, Axelrod joined the National Institute for Mental Health, where his study of neurotransmission of adrenaline and amphetamines led to his investigative studies of psychoactive drugs for the treatment of mental illnesses, especially schizophrenia. He shares the 1970 Nobel Prize in physiology for his work on chemical neurotransmission and pharmacological interactions.

Julius Axelrod

To achieve excellence in scientific
research, one must be highly motivated,
exercise good judgment, have imagination,
determination, money, luck and
the ability to ask the right
questions at the right time.

Julius Axelrod
Nobel Laureate in
Physiology or Medicine

120

GEORGE A. OLAH
Winner of the Nobel Prize in chemistry, 1994

Excellence is an exceptional effort or achievement of highest standard or merit. It is best to leave evaluation of such to someone's peers in a sufficient historical perspective to avoid premature or biased judgments.

Born in Budapest, Hungary, in 1927, George Olah immigrated to Canada then to the United States where he worked as a research scientist. Olah's pioneering research focused on hydrocarbon molecules, leading to improved energy sources and earning him the Nobel Prize.

GEORGE A. OLAH

Excellence is an exceptional effort or achievement of highest standard or merit. It is best to leave evaluation of such to someones peers in a sufficient historical perspective to avoid premature or biased judgement

Geo. Olah

1994 NOBEL LAUREATE IN CHEMISTRY

121
RICHARD SAUL WURMAN
Author; designer; architect

> My expertise has always been my ignorance—my admission
> and my acceptance of not knowing. My work and ideas
> come from the question—not from the answer.

With the publication of his first book in 1962 at the age of twenty-six, Richard Saul Wurman began the singular passion in his life: that of making information understandable. His many best-selling books come from his desire to know, rather than from already knowing, he says, from his ignorance rather than his intelligence, from his inability rather than his ability. He coined the phrase "information architecture" and created the T.E.D. Conferences, bringing together the fields of Technology, Entertainment, and Design.

Richard Saul Wurman

My expertise has always been
my ignorance — my admission
& my acceptance of not
knowing. My work & ideas
come from the question
— not from the answer

[signature]

122

RABBI ALEXANDER M. SCHINDLER
Religious leader; president of the Union of American Hebrew Congregations

"To get to Carnegie Hall—practice—practice!"

———————

Rabbi Alexander Schindler was committed to a Judaism that embraced the cause of social justice, and he spoke out forcefully for the poor, for civil rights, and for gay and lesbian rights. Schindler died in 2000, leaving millions touched and inspired with his love, his humor, his charisma, and his optimism for the future.

RABBI ALEXANDER M. SCHINDLER ● UNION OF AMERICAN HEBREW CONGREGATIONS
PRESIDENT

"To get to Carnegie Hall
-- practice -- practice!"

123
LEON N. COOPER
Winner of the Nobel Prize in physics, 1972

Excellence requires hard work. We all know that. But often fun takes work too: sailing, skiing, playing or listening to music require effort to develop our skills as well as our taste. Instant cinema is for the movies.

A physicist born in New York City, Leon Cooper collaborated with John Bardeen and John Robert Schrieffer to develop the BCS (Bardeen, Cooper, Schrieffer) theory of superconductivity, which won the three scientists the 1972 Nobel Prize in physics. He began teaching at Brown University in 1958, where he predicted the low-temperature pairing of electrons now known in the scientific world as Cooper Pairs. His later investigations have led to breakthroughs on memory organization studies of the brain.

BROWN UNIVERSITY
Providence, Rhode Island 02912

Leon N Cooper
Thomas J. Watson, Sr.
Professor of Science

Director, Institute for Brain and Neural Systems

Excellence requires hard work.
We all know that. But often fun
takes work too: sailing, skiing, playing
or listening to music require effort to
develop our skills as well as our taste.
Instant cinema is for the movies.

Leon N Cooper

124
RUDOLPH E. TANZI, PH.D.
Medical researcher; professor of Neurology at Harvard Medical School

Excellence begins with looking inward. It endures by staying true to yourself and, in the end, excellence saves mankind.

Rudolph Tanzi is leading research to dissect the genetics of Alzheimer's disease. His work will be invaluable for the development of therapies and treatments for this condition, and will spare millions of individuals and their families the heartache and suffering that accompanies the debilitating disease.

HARVARD MEDICAL SCHOOL ◆ MASSACHUSETTS GENERAL HOSPITAL

RUDOLPH E. TANZI, Ph.D.
Assoc. Professor of Neurology
Harvard Medical School

Director,
Genetics and Aging Unit 1496101
Neurology Service
Neuroscience Center
Massachusetts General Hospital

Excellence begins with looking inward.
It endures by staying true to yourself
And, in the end, excellence serves mankind

Rudolph E. Tanzi

125
JAMES A. VAN ALLEN
Astronomy pioneer; scientist; professor

> Excellence is the product of patience, persistence, and rigorous attention to detail in pursuit of an objective.

Using data from the *Explorer I* and *Pioneer III* space probes of the region known as the magnetosphere, James Van Allen discovered the existence of the radiation belts. These concentrations of electrically charged particles, known since his discovery as the Van Allen Belts, are one of the most dramatic discoveries of the century.

Excellence is the
product of patience,
persistence, and rigorous
attention to detail in
pursuit of an objective.

James A. Van Allen
Professor of Physics

126

JAMES TOBIN
Winner of the Nobel Prize in economics, 1981

> Time is short. Pursue your own interests, your own curiosities. Think things out for yourself. Don't be afraid to question accepted views. Keep your priorities straight. Be generous to your elders, your teachers, your co-workers, for "if you see farther, it is because you stand on the shoulders of giants."

James Tobin was a member of President Kennedy's Council of Economic Advisors in 1961 and 1962, and was awarded the Nobel Prize in economics. Tobin has said that his ongoing interest in economics is derived from his belief that the improved understanding of economics could better mankind and our communities around the globe.

Yale University

Cowles Foundation for Research
in Economics
Department of Economics

Time is short. Pursue your own
interests, your own curiosities. Think
things out for yourself. Don't be afraid to
question accepted views. Keep your
priorities straight. Be generous to your
elders, your teachers, your co-workers, for
"if you see farther, it is because you
stand on the shoulders of giants".

James Tobin

127

GEORGE C. WALLACE
Governor of Alabama

Believe in yourself and what you are doing and never,
never, never give up.

In 1963, as governor of Alabama, George Wallace stood in the door-
way of the administration building of the University of Alabama, deny-
ing two black students admission. Later in life Wallace accepted that
his beliefs were wrong, publicly admitted so, asked for forgiveness,
then aggressively fought for equal rights. African American leaders
ultimately embraced Wallace as an important and courageous example of how any person can let go of hatred and prejudice and
embrace love and fairness to all.

Believe in yourself
and what you are
doing & mean, never
never give up.
Gov. G. Wallace

128
GARY S. BECKER
Winner of the Nobel Prize in Economics, 1992

To achieve excellence requires taking risks of failure, and inner strength to pursue an idea or other goals despite criticism.

Considered to be one of the sharpest economic minds ever, Gary Becker has often challenged the accepted economic theories and introduced original ideas into the economic community. He taught at Columbia University, then at the University of Chicago. His controversial ideas on labor discrimination, division of labor within the family, and crime as an economic career choice have challenged the economic community and continue to effect economic models today.

GARY S. BECKER
University Professor of Economics and Sociology

To achieve excellence requires taking risks of failure, and inner strength to pursue an idea or other goals despite criticism.

Gary S. Becker

129

BROOKE BENNETT
Olympic athlete; gold medalist, swimming, 1996, 2000

My thoughts come from my grandfather who started me swimming. He died shortly before the Olympics. I dedicated my race to him and I dedicate this writing to him. Thanks, "Dad," so much for your love for me and swimming. Thanks so much for teaching me to be tough and to never say I can't. You taught me not to cry when I got beat in a race but to get back in and win the next time!

Brooke Bennett was only sixteen years old when she won a gold medal in the 800 freestyle swim at the Atlanta Olympics. She repeated in the 2000 Sydney Olympics with gold medals in the 400 and 800 meter freestyle races.

My thoughts come from my grandfather who started me swimming. He died shortly before the Olympics. I dedicated my race to him & I dedicate this writing to him.

Thanks "Dad" so much for your love for me & swimming. Thanks so much for teaching me to be tough & to never say I can't. You taught me not to cry when I got beat in a race but to get back in & win the next time!

130

MARTIN RODBELL, PH.D.
Winner of the Nobel Prize in physiology or medicine, 1994

> Excellence is a relative matter largely dependent on one's
> cultural environment. In many respects, my scientific career
> and my experiences with people and events have been
> seamless in that I cannot separate one from another.
> Without doubt, the thread of one's life should be within the
> matrix of the total human experience.

———————————

In 1994, Martin Rodbell shared the Nobel Prize in physiology or medicine with Alfred G. Gilman for his work in discovering G-proteins, substances that help transmit chemical signals in cells that control fundamental life processes: too many or too few G-proteins can lead to diseases ranging from alcoholism and cholera to diabetes and cancer. His work in this area contributed to the prevention and treatment of these diseases, enabling longer lives for people around the globe. Rodbell died in 1998.

Martin Rodbell, Ph.D
Nobel Laureate in Medicine or Physiology, 1994

Excellence is a relative matter largely dependent on one's cultural environment. In many respects, my scientific career and my experiences with people and events have been seamless in that I cannot separate one from another. Without doubt, the thread of one's life should be within the matrix of the total human experience.

Martin Rodbell

131
ROD STEIGER
Actor; Academy Award winner, Best Actor, 1967

To cry is the instant release but to cry and not to gain is complete defeat. Pain is a teacher that must be understood.

———————

Rod Steiger is probably best known for his role in *On the Waterfront* in 1954. Later films include *Al Capone* (1958), *Dr. Zhivago* (1965), *The Pawnbroker* (1965), and *In the Heat of the Night*, for which he won an Oscar in 1967. However, his newest role is highly personal. Finally free of the chronic depression that plagued him for over eight years, Steiger has become a powerful advocate for the rights and acceptance of the mentally ill.

To cry is the instant release

BUT

To cry and not to gain is
complete
DEFEAT.

Pain is a teacher that must
be
Understood.

Rod Steiger

132

BETSY ALISON
Champion sailor; Olympic coach

> Practice and preparation are keys to success. We like to practice what we're good at, and hate to practice what we're weak in. Each time we master a weakness, it becomes another "tool" in the toolbox, and once we have all the necessary tools the potential for building success is unlimited.

Betsy Alison was named Coach of the Year by the U.S. Olympic Committee and, as a competitor, was awarded the Rolex Yachtswoman of the Year Award an unprecedented five times. Alison also provides extraordinary leadership in sports for the disabled, having launched a training program for U.S. disabled sailors that helped them win the world championship and earn the United States a berth in Sydney, where paralympic sailing made its debut as a full medal sport.

Betsy Alison

Practice and preparation are keys to success. We like to practice what we're good at, and hate to practice what we're weak in. Each time we master a weakness, it becomes another 'tool' in the toolbox, and once we have all the necessary tools the potential for building success is unlimited!

Betsy Alison

133
GEORGE WALKER
Winner of the Pulitzer Prize in Music, 1996

> Excellence is the by-product of many factors that include talent, motivation, preparation, dedication, determination, emulation and imagination.

George Walker started playing the piano at age five and began composing at age eighteen. He was the first African American to win the prestigious Pulitzer Prize in Music. He won for composition of "Lilacs," a piece for voice and orchestra, which premiered on February 1, 1996, with the Boston Symphony Orchestra.

Excellence is the by-products of many factors that include talent, motivation, preparation, dedication, determination, emulation and imagination.

CHAPTER FIVE

Leadership

134
ELIE WIESEL
Winner of the Nobel Peace Prize, 1986

Wherever men or women are persecuted because of their race, religion or political views, that place must—at that moment—become the center of the universe.

———————

A writer born in Sighet, Romania, Elie Wiesel was taken, at the age of sixteen, to Nazi concentration camps. Nearly his entire family died at Auschwitz and Buchenwald. His life has been devoted to writing and speaking about the Holocaust, with the aim of making sure that it is not forgotten. In 1986, Wiesel received the Nobel Peace Prize for his work as a "messenger to mankind."

Boston University

Elie Wiesel, *Andrew W. Mellon Professor in the Humanities*

Wherever men or women are persecuted because of their race, religion or political views, that place must - at that moment - become the center of the universe.

Elie Wiesel

135

GEORGE T. MCDONALD
Community leader; founder, the Doe Fund

A good leader equips people to care for themselves.

George McDonald got tired of stepping over and around homeless men and women on the streets of New York on his way to work, to lunch, to his apartment. He decided that there must be something that he could do to change the fact that hundreds of homeless people literally lay in his path each and every day, while he went on with his very successful business and personal life. So, McDonald founded the Doe Fund, Inc., and Ready, Willing, and Able. Based in New York City, his organization has helped hundreds of homeless men and women achieve lives of independence and self-sufficiency.

A Good Leader Equips
people To Care
For Others So level.

George McDonald

136

DONNA E. SHALALA
Cabinet secretary to President Clinton, Health and Human Services Department

> True leaders aren't judged by college degrees, but by character. They aren't judged by what they earn, but by what they contribute. And they aren't judged by who they know, but by who they are.

———————

Donna E. Shalala joined the Clinton-Gore administration in January 1993, and was the longest serving secretary of Health and Human Services in U.S. history, overseeing a budget of approximately $387 billion and more than 61,000 employees. Shalala redefined the role of HHS secretary, partnering with businesses, the media, and other private sector organizations to extend the department's public health and education mission.

True leaders aren't judged by
college degrees, but by character.
They aren't judged by what they
earn, but by what they contribute.
And they aren't judged by who
they know, but by who they are."

D E Sell

137

GERRY SPENCE
Lawyer; media commentator

> Any great leader listens, knows his limitations and cherishes the insights and creativity offered up by those he leads. Then, having disposed of his own ego, like a child picking precious shells on the beach, he sorts through them and keeps the best.

Gerry Spence has a conducted a national law practice and has tried and won some of America's most famous cases. Observers contend that Spence's court work has changed the face of trial law in America. His continuing agenda is to promote justice in America for the average person and to make the American system one that serves the average citizen.

Any great leader listens, knows his limitations and cherishes the insights and creativity offered up by those he leads. Then, having disposed of his own ego, like a child picking precious shells on the beach, he sorts through them and keeps the best.

Gerry Spence

138
WILMA MANKILLER
Native American leader

> A positive outlook is the greatest attribute a leader can possess. I begin my prayers with a request that all negative thoughts be removed from my mind.

While commuting to the University of Arkansas to complete her graduate studies, Wilma Mankiller suffered a near-fatal head-on car accident. In an effort to recover from her injuries, she adopted her Cherokee tradition of "being of good mind." This tradition, the ability to think positively and transform situations into better paths, has been the backbone to her community service. In 1987, she was elected the first woman principal chief of the Cherokee Nation and in 1998 was awarded the presidential Medal of Freedom.

WILMA MANKILLER

A positive outlook is the greatest attribute a leader can possess. I begin my prayers with a request that all negative thoughts be removed from my mind.

Wilma
Mankiller

139
FRANK BORMAN
Astronaut; business leader

Stay in there and pitch!

One of America's earliest astronauts, Frank Borman was commander of the fourteen-day *Gemini VII* mission, which performed the first space rendezvous, and commander of *Apollo 8,* which was the first spacecraft to orbit the Moon. While orbiting the Moon on Christmas Eve, 1968, and relaying television pictures of its rugged surface, the crew captivated millions of viewers by reading from the Bible's Book of Genesis. Borman later served as CEO of Eastern Airlines.

Stay in there,
and pitch!

Frank Borman

140

ALAN KHAZEI
Community leader; cofounder, City Year

> We must remember that all great change begins with an
> idealistic notion. It is the voice that says sometimes simply,
> sometimes movingly, sometimes inspiringly, often quietly,
> "Things aren't what they *could* be. Things aren't what they
> *should* be. We *can* do better, and we *must* try."

Alan Khazei is a change agent and has built a strong vehicle for
social change in the United States. His brainchild, City Year, is a
domestic Peace Corps–type organization that he cofounded with law
school friend Michael Brown in 1988. The program has grown from
fifty members in Boston, where they began, to more than a thousand
members in eleven cities. City Year seeks to inspire people to engage
in a lifetime commitment to service.

Alan Khazei
Co-Founder

**NATIONAL
HEADQUARTERS**

We must remember that all great change begins with an idealistic notion. It is the voice that says sometimes simply, sometimes movingly, sometimes inspiringly, other quietly, "Things aren't what they could be. Things aren't what they should be. We can do better and we must try."

BOSTON

CHICAGO

CLEVELAND

COLUMBIA

COLUMBUS

RHODE ISLAND

SAN ANTONIO

SAN JOSE

NATIONAL SPONSORS

digital

Timberland

PUTTING IDEALISM TO WORK

141
KATHLEEN KENNEDY TOWNSEND
Political leader; lieutenant governor of Maryland

> The most important thing I know is that you must love
> those you want to lead.

———————

The eldest child of Robert and Ethel Kennedy, Democratic Lieutenant Governor Kathleen Kennedy Townsend's core mission is to make Maryland's communities safer, stronger, and more prosperous with innovative, effective answers to the state's most critical challenges.

OFFICE OF
THE LT. GOVERNOR
STATE HOUSE
ANNAPOLIS, MARYLAND 21401

KATHLEEN KENNEDY TOWNSEND
LT. GOVERNOR

The most important thing
I know is that you must
love those you want to lead.

Kathleen Kennedy
Townsend

142

JEAN-MICHEL COUSTEAU
Oceanographer

People protect what they love.

Jean-Michel Cousteau has spent his life with his family exploring the world's oceans aboard the research vessels *Calypso* and *Alcyone*, communicating to people of all nations and generations his love and concern for our planet. He formed Ocean Futures to provide a comprehensive information resource, conduct education programs, develop marine education programs, and foster a conservation ethic in our children for the preservation of our water planet.

Ocean Futures

Jean-Michel Cousteau · Keiko

People protect what they
love.

Jean Cousteau

143
ARN CHORN-POND
Cambodian refugee leader

There is a common ground of suffering between all of us in the world. It seems almost unbelievable that I could forgive what happened to my people. Two million Cambodians and one million children died in my country during the period of Pol Pot, the Killing Field, but more and more I realize I'm alive. Not just because bullets failed to reach my brain, or because I wasn't butchered in the awful Cambodian genocide; I'm alive, really only painfully, after all these years, because I love again. I can feel the suffering of others, not just my own, who are enduring the violence of human madness. To be a good leader, you must understand this and have compassion.

Arn Chorn-Pond's entire family was killed by the Khmer Rouge of Cambodia. Taken from his parents at the age of eight, he was held prisoner, where it became his job to play the flute, every day for two years, while the Khmer Rouge executed prisoners. He escaped his captors, attended Brown University, and in 1992 returned to Cambodia and founded a youth group that now has sixty thousand members working for peace.

There is a common ground of suffering between all of us in the world. It seems almost unbelievable that I could forgive what happened to my people 2 million Cambodians and one million children died in my country during the period of Pol Pot the Killing Fields, but more and more I realize I'm alive. Not just because bullets failed to reach my brain, or because I wasn't butchered in the awful Cambodian genocide; I'm alive, really only painfully, after all these years, because I love again. I can feel the suffering of others, not just my own, who are enduring the violence of human madness. To be a good leader, you must understand this and have compassion.

Arn Chorn-Pond
a Cambodian orphan.

144

FRANCES HESSELBEIN
Founding president, the Drucker Foundation

A Personal Definition of Leadership: "Leadership is a matter of how to be, not how to do it."

———————————

Frances Hesselbein received the presidential Medal of Freedom, the nation's highest civilian honor, in recognition of her leadership as CEO of Girl Scouts of the U.S.A. and of her role in leading charitable organizations toward performance excellence. Hesselbein, through the Drucker Foundation, has used her expertise to serve as a broker of intellectual capital, bringing together the finest thought leaders in the world with the leaders of charitable organizations, in order to advance the many missions addressing community needs.

The Drucker Foundation

Frances Hesselbein
Chairman
Board of Governors

A Personal Definition of
Leadership

" Leadership is a matter
of how to be, not
how to do it. "

Frances Hesselbein

145

JOSEPH P. KENNEDY II

U.S. congressman; social entrepreneur

> The person who says it cannot be done should not interrupt
> the person doing it!!

Joe Kennedy, eldest son of the late Senator Robert F. Kennedy, served for six terms as U.S. Congressman from Massachusetts, representing the same district that his uncle, John F. Kennedy, had served in the late 1940s. He left Congress and returned to Citizens Energy Corporation, the nonprofit agency he founded nearly two decades ago to provide heating assistance to the poor. During his tenure as a congressman, he worked on such issues as health care, affordable housing, Social Security, Medicare, and educational opportunities for young and old alike.

The person who says it cannot
be done
   Should not interrupt the
person doing it !!

JOSEPH P. KENNEDY II
MEMBER OF CONGRESS
WASHINGTON, D. C. 20515

146

NANCY BRINKER
Cancer cure leader

> The most important thing I have learned is that people only give to people—not causes, not institutions, not governments—only to people who inspire their generosity.

Nancy Brinker established the Susan G. Komen Breast Cancer Foundation in 1982 to honor her sister, Susan Komen, who died of breast cancer at age thirty-six, leaving behind her husband and two young children. Today, the Komen Foundation sponsors "Race for the Cure" events across the country and is the nation's largest private funder of research dedicated solely to breast cancer research, education, screening, and treatment.

Nancy Brinker

The most important thing I have learned is that people only give to people — not causes, not institutions, not governments — only to people who inspire their generosity.

Nan Brinker

147

WENDY KOPP
Teaching leader; founder, Teach for America

There is nothing more important when pursuing a mission than being surrounded by talented people you can trust.

While still a senior at Princeton and troubled by the inequities in America's educational system, Wendy Kopp became determined to start a movement of recent college graduates to effect change in urban and rural public schools. This movement, she planned, would not only change the lives of thousands of underserved students but would also shape the priorities of all who took part. Teach for America became Kopp's brainchild, inspiring six thousand outstanding individuals to change the lives of nearly half a million children and commit to being lifelong leaders in the fight for true educational equality.

One day, all children in this nation will have the opportunity to attain an excellent education.

There's nothing more important when pursuing a mission than being surrounded by talented people you can trust.

Wendy Kopp

148
LONNIE R. BRISTOW, M.D.
Medical industry leader

> In the face of opposition that can seem so overwhelmingly
> negative at times; in the face of hatred, prejudice and
> outright evil itself; in the face of all these forces, holds firm
> my faith that the majesty of the human spirit will ultimately
> triumph in the end—and that America is a nation of great
> passion which is trying, almost desperately at times, to
> achieve the added and redeeming quality of compassion.

After many years of leadership in organized medicine and as
President of the AMA, Lonnie Bristow now devotes his time to advocacy of public health issues and improving our nation's health policy.
Bristow serves as a director of the American Legacy Foundation,
which is the largest effort focused entirely on the problems associ-
ated with tobacco use, our nation's single most preventable cause of
death.

In the face of opposition that can seem so overwhelmingly negative at times; in the face of hatred, prejudice and outright evil itself; in the face of all these forces, holds firm my faith that the majesty of the human spirit will ultimately treumph in the end — and that America is a nation of great Passion which is trying, almost desperately at times, to achieve the added and redeeming quality of Compassion.

Lonnie R. Bristow MD

149
ANN M. FUDGE
Business leader

> You are a child of the universe; no less than the trees and
> the stars you have a right to be here. And whether or not it
> is clear to you, no doubt the universe is unfolding as it
> should.

> —(*From* Desiderata)

Ann M. Fudge is an extraordinary leader in business and philan-
thropy. She was named by *Fortune* magazine as one of the fifty most
powerful women in American business. Fudge earned her B.A. from
Simmons College and her M.B.A. from Harvard Business School and
firmly believes that things will unfold for each person as they are
intended to, but that we must participate in order to better our own
life and the lives of those around us.

You are a child of the universe;
No less than the trees and the
stars you have a right to be
here. And whether or not it is
clear to you, no doubt the
universe is unfolding as it should.

from Desiderata

150
MICHAEL S. DUKAKIS
Democratic nominee for president, 1988

> It was my parents who used to say to me: "Much has been given to you, and much is expected of you."

Michael Dukakis served as governor of Massachusetts, leading the state to be dubbed the "Massachusetts Miracle" in recognition of the state's extraordinary economic advances. His leadership as governor enabled him to win the Democratic Party's nomination for president in 1988. Dukakis lost the election to George Bush, but continued his public service as a member of the faculty of several colleges, including Northeastern, Harvard's Kennedy School of Government, and UCLA.

It was my parents who used to say to me:
"Much has been given to you; and much is expected of you."

Barbara Jordan

151
RICHARD H. TRULY
Astronaut; space pioneer

> My days in America's space program made me appreciate these words by Goethe: "Whatever you do or dream you can, begin it. Boldness has genius, power and magic in it."

Richard H. Truly became NASA's associate administrator for space flight in 1986. In this position, he led the painstaking rebuilding of the Space Shuttle program in the wake of the *Challenger* disaster. With a stellar history of flight and space missions, Truly has earned universal admiration and was awarded the presidential Citizen's Medal by President Reagan.

Richard H. Truly
Vice President
Director, **Georgia Tech Research Institute**

My days in America's Space program made me appreciate these words by Goethe:

"Whatever you do or dream you can, begin it. Boldness has genius, power and magic in it."

Richard Truly

152

GLORIA FELDT
President, Planned Parenthood; women's advocate

> The world turns on human connections. Timing is the next
> most important thing. And the resources we need are
> always there if we can but see them.

Gloria Feldt is president of Planned Parenthood Federation of America, the nation's oldest and largest reproductive heath care and advocacy organization. She has established herself as a leading national voice for family planning, reproductive choice, and responsible sex education, and she was named by *Vanity Fair* magazine as one of America's Top 200 Women Leaders, Legends, and Trailblazers.

The world turns on human connections,
Timing is the next most important thing.
And the resources we need are always
there if we can but see them.

Gloria Feldt

153

SHELDON L. GLASHOW
Winner of the Nobel Prize in physics, 1979

Each of us should strive to improve human welfare, or in some other manner, to leave the world a better place. My own goal has been to understand just a tiny bit more about the wonders of nature.

A winner of the Nobel Prize in physics, Sheldon Glashow's first taste of science took place in the basement laboratory his dad built for him, where he explored the world of chemistry and biology and played with frogs. He is continually challenged and excited by the still unanswered questions in science, the theories that still need to be refined. In his autobiography, *Intentions,* Glashow writes, "Can anyone really believe that nature's bag of tricks has run out? . . . Of course not. Let the show go on!"

Each of us should strive to improve human welfare, or in some other manner, to leave the world a better place. My own goal has been to understand just a tiny bit more about the wonders of Nature.

Sheldon Lee Glashow

154
WALTER CRONKITE
Newscaster

Leaders have the courage to hold fast to their principles
when expediency seems to demand otherwise.

————————————

Walter Cronkite is perhaps the most beloved journalist in America. He
reported from the European front during World War II, helped launch
the *CBS Evening News* in 1962, has been an eloquent and forceful
supporter of environmental causes, and is widely admired for his
honesty, objectivity, and levelheaded reporting.

Leaders have the courage to hold
fast to their principles when expediency seems
to demand otherwise.

Walter Cronkite

LECH WALESA

Winner of the Nobel Peace Prize, 1983; former president of Poland

> I had only two things, belief in God and belief in what
> I was doing.

Lech Walesa was born in 1943. He was an auto mechanic, served in the army, then joined the Gdansk shipyards as an electrician. In 1978, he began organizing non-Communist trade unions, and in August 1980 led the Gdansk shipyard strike to advance workers' rights. The strike led to a national labor movement and contributed to the downfall of communism. In 1983, he was awarded the Nobel Peace Prize, and in 1990, he was elected president of Poland. I asked him why he has hope for a better future and what one needs to contribute to that future . . .

Miałem tylko dwie
rzeczy - wiarę w Boga
i w to, co robię

Contributors